Dog People Are Crazy

Consisting Chiefly Of The Innocently
Asked And Outrageously Funny Inquiries
To a Dog Editor And His Irreverent
Replies; Plus Divers Wildly Absurd
Incidents Connected With Dogs And
Doggy People: All Indecorously Recorded
By The Craziest Doggist Of Them
All—MAXWELL RIDDLE

D1564558

1981
New Expanded Edition
Third Printing
HOWELL BOOK HOUSE INC.
230 Park Avenue
New York, N.Y. 10169

ISBN 0-87605-536-6

Contents

Foreword

A lady called to get information before purchasing her first dog. Some of her questions required frank and direct answers. She was somewhat shocked.

"I'm convinced," she said, "that all dog people are crazy, and that you're the craziest one of all."

"Madam," I replied, "now we understand each other, for I admit the charge. But, if you get into dogs, you'll end up just as crazy as the rest of us."

I was wrong. The lady is now trying to recreate the extinct Asian Five Pinks dog, and she's even nuttier than the rest of us.

All of the incidents herewith recorded are true. Most of them are taken from thousands of inquiries made to the author in his capacity as a dog columnist. Some are experiences which occurred at dog shows, or field trials, or upon other occasions when doggy people joyfully congregate.

A most cynical and observant person, which is to say the author himself, has noted that all conversations about dogs work around to problems of feeding and sex. Wherefore, the author begs the liberty of his dear readers to begin with feeding, while hoping that the beginning, if more decorous than the ending, will be no less titillating to the risibilities of those who enter herewith the zany world of dogdom.

Maxwell Riddle

About the Author

MAXWELL RIDDLE is a mental giant, a dynamo in physical energy—and virtually omniscient in dog lore. In quality, number and versatility, his accomplishments as an authority on dogs are unparalleled among his contemporaries in the field.

He has owned, bred and shown many breeds. His judging assignments, covering all breeds, have taken him into six world areas: America, Canada, Australia, Africa, Asia and South America. His weekly column was syndicated for many years in *The New York Post* and other newspapers in the U.S.A.; he has written a dozen dog books; he contributed more than half the articles in *The International Encyclopedia of Dogs*; and he is an associate editor of *Dog World* and contributor to other magazines.

Past President of the Dog Writers' Association of America, he has won *all* of the Association's journalism awards, to which he is eligible, for excellence in writing, many of them two to four times. In 1973, after many terms of office, he retired as President of the Ravenna Kennel Club which he also served as show chairman for 34 years.He has also served as President and show chairman of the Western Reserve Kennel Club of Cleveland.

In *Dog People Are Crazy* Mr. Riddle presents the lighter side of his unequalled career in the world of dogs and their owners. Every letter and every doggy incident reported in this incredibly amusing book are true. In this new, expanded edition the writer has added many real-life anecdotes including those derived more recently from his experiences as an internationally famous dog judge.

In the more serious vein, Mr. Riddle continues to write the most helpful advice in print to dog owners everywhere. Currently he is engaged also in compiling a masterwork on the wonderful world of the wild dogs.

1

Dog Feeding

TEA AND CRUMPETS ANYONE?

Dog feeding is the most controversial subject in dogdom. And no one in his right mind would follow the instructions of a specialist, a successful dog breeder, or a dog food manufacturer. Your own ideas will always be better. The dogs will adjust themselves to your system, and this will prove you right. Or, if they die of your methods, this will be hard to prove, and you can always blame that neighbor you don't like, claiming he put out rat poison.

During World War II, *The Cleveland Press* printed a coupon along with its dog column, and asked readers to fill in the blanks. Did they feed canned food exclusively, meal type, biscuits, horse meat? Or combinations of these?

Practically no one filled in the blanks. But hundreds wrote long letters, outlining in detail their feeding methods and their pet theories. Here are some of them.

Dear Sir:

I have a 12 year old Chow, and he is in perfect condition, which is because of the way I feed him.

Breakfast: On Monday, corn flakes and milk with a poached egg on top. Tuesdays and Thursdays, hot cooked cereal with soft boiled egg. Other mornings, shredded wheat with milk and poached egg.

Lunch: Warm milk and Graham crackers. Sometimes soup.

Supper: Kibbled biscuit with cooked vegetables, including their juices, and calves liver, or kidney.

Fortunately I have never had to resort to such terrible things as horse meat. And I never would. I think I would put Chintzie to sleep before making him eat horse meat.

Sincerely,
Mr. _____

Dear Sir:

. . . and I have noticed that dogs like to eat horse manure.

Now I keep a supply of it handy, drying it carefully. I add it to kibbled biscuits, horse meat, and hot water. My dogs thrive on it. I've never had a case of distemper since I started to use it, and I'm sure this is the reason.

Sincerely,

J. W. _____

If you'll eliminate all that other stuff you mention, you'll prove that like the horse and the sparrow, two CAN live as cheap as one.

Dear Sir:

Our Coonhounds got terribly sick once, and everyone said they were going to die. I let them out, and they began to eat off a patch of grass. Right of way, they both got well. So now we raise grass specially for the dogs.

In summer we feed it fresh. In the fall, we mow it and dry it for winter use. But we are careful to soak it before adding it to the food.

We haven't had a case of distemper since we started to feed grass. And we're certain this is the reason.

Sincerely,

T. R. _____

Lo, the poor carnivore become like Nebuchadnezzar, a grass lands grazer.

Dear Sir:

Our Mike is in perfect condition even at the age of 15. I attribute this mostly to his diet. Meat makes a dog mean, and we don't feed it. Our Mike gets shredded wheat, poached egg, and milk for breakfast. For supper, we cook spinach, cabbage, carrots, and Navy beans for him, and we add hot corn meal muffins to this.

This makes him a little gassy, but I think it is good for him. I've noticed that gassy people seem to be healthier than others.

Sincerely,

Mrs. _____

Or more successful. Consider all the senators down in Washington.

Dear Sir:

   . . . A dog is human and likes what we like. Our poodles get pork chops every Saturday night.

Sincerely,

Miss _____

If it's true that Poodles were once used for truffle snuffling, why not truffles and champagne?

Dear Sir:

   I am English, and as such, I adhere to the old English custom of tea and cookies in the afternoon. My dogs love this custom, too. I have chairs especially for them. I give them warm, unsweetened tea, so as not to spoil their evening meal.

   My dogs have never had distemper. And I'm convinced that this is the reason why. Also, I believe that tea and crumpets keep my dogs' eyes clear, and their coats shining.

Sincerely,

Col. J. A. _____

Tea and strumpets have made many an Englishman happy, but we don't know about the distemper.

Dear Sir:

   I wonder if you could help me cure loose bowels in my dog. He is a Scottie, two years old, and we have given him nothing but the best of loving care. Yet he has loose bowels and is thin.

   We wouldn't dream of feeding him one of those horrible dog foods. We've had him since he was four weeks old, and we have fed him nothing but diluted milk and the richest soups.

Sincerely,

H. A. _____

Possibly a cracker in the soup would give a firmer stool!

8

HE JUST WON'T EAT DOG FOOD.

Dear Sir:

I read your article, but I didn't see any sense in filling out that coupon. I guess I just need some help. My puppy is now 15 months old, and he seems hungry all the time. Like the fellow said that gave him to us, when he was three weeks old, we feed him Pablum and milk five times a day.

But why is he always hungry? Is he still too young to have dog food or milk? Will meat give him worms? Please send me all the answers to these and other problems.

Sincerely,
Mrs. _____

Lady, did you nurse your baby until he was 21 years old?

Dear Sir:

I saw your coupon in the paper, and there is no need for me to fill it out. Cause I don't think you need my help. But maybe you can help me.

I got a Coonhound, as fine a running dog as you ever seed. Trouble is, he ain't got much of a voice. And though you can hear him blatting on the trail pretty good, the other hunters got to calling him squeaky. I don't like this no how, calling a good cooner such a name.

So now what I want to know, is there some food I can feed him will give him a real booming voice, like the kind of dog he really is. And also, I don't want the boys knowing I writ to you. So answer confidential.

Your humble svt.,
Ezra D

Try feeding him bay leaves!

10

Dear Sir:

Now I filled out that coupon like you asked, but it's not what I feed my dog, but what she eats by herself.

Twice she has et up one or more of the kids mittens, and once a real nice sweater, and another time one of my husband's wool hunting socks.

Now what I'm wondering, does that dog have one of them hidden hungers the radio people keep yelping about? If so, should I try feeding that dog a little wool at each meal?

I don't think so, because that wool never does seem to get digested. The vet has had to go in there with some tongs sort of things, and drag out all that stuff, and it sure don't look like it was digested any.

I asked the vet, and he scratched his head, but he never did give no answer. So what do you say?

Sincerely,
Mrs.———

I scratch, too. In any case, if it doesn't kill her first, she'll get over the habit.

Dear Sir:

I have a dog problem, and maybe you can help me with it. Our dog was a big old mongrel, and it bit the neighborhood children. So we had it destroyed. Then we got this Doberman Pinscher, which we dearly love. And he is as gentle as can be.

But the trouble with him, he's gassy. It's bad enough when we're alone with him. But it is most embarrassing when we have company, and he goes bloom and then there is that horrible smell.

What is even worse, he likes to sleep with my wife and me. And we let him do it on Sunday mornings when we don't have to get up early. He gets down under the covers, right between us. And then bloom and we are blasted right out of bed by that terrible smell.

What do you suggest?

Sincerely,
A. H. S.

Try going to early church on Sunday mornings.

Dear Sir:

My dog has the queerest eating habits, and I wonder if you think he is normal.

Once he ate a pack of cigarettes (king size with filter tips), and including the package. This made him so sick at his stomach he didn't die from it.

Then a couple of weeks ago, he ate a match booklet. This nearly did kill him, and it cost me $23 at the vet hospital to get him well. The vet said he would have died if I hadn't seen him finishing off those matches and rushed him right over there.

Another time, he ate my son's sock. And then one day my husband's muffler. The vet had to reach in and pull that out with forceps. Another big hospital bill!

On the other hand, he won't even chase a cat. Is this normal? I forgot to say he is a mixed breed. Could it be that being a cur has sort of given him a phobia, and he takes off the pressure in this way?

Yours very truly,

Mrs. ――――――

Whatever his trouble, the neighborhood cats must love him.

Dear Sir:

I have a dog 13 weeks old. When can I start giving her water? I was told water would give her diarrhoea. I give her milk, and baby cereals, and raw eggs. And she has the diarrhoea anyway. So when can I give her water? And is it necessary to boil it first? I was told she would get worms if I gave her milk. And I think she has worms. So shall I stop giving her milk?

Sincerely,

Mrs. ――――――

And the dog lived!

Note: Millions of people claim milk will give a dog worms. They never ask themselves why it should give worms to dogs and not to humans and tends to rob dogs of certain vitamins.

Dear Mr. Ridell:

Six months ago we bought a cockerel Spaniel Puppy. At that time, his head was smooth, and he had short hair. We was told he was a pure breed, and papered. Now he has a top knot of long, curly hair. What is wrong? Did we get kedaddled, or are we feeding him wrong? How come that top knot?

Awaiting your answer,

Joe J _____

My mother done told me I was born bald.

Reminiscence

Sometimes dogs make monkeys out of dog writers, including this one. It is well to admit this, so that we can leave this chapter on even terms; you, dear readers, the seekers of advice, and I, the expert whose advice is ignored.

All writers warn against feeding fowl and chop bones to dogs. The fowl bones may splinter and puncture the throat or stomach. The steak bones may be broken up by the dog's strong teeth, then can become impacted in the intestines.

Now, of course, dogs don't read the dog columns, nor do they listen to the experts. This was the case with our retired racing Greyhound, Fawn. Fawn came home from the tracks; sat on my wife's royal blue rug, and looked like a golden dog of Egyptian tomb statuary. He seemed a perfect gentleman.

But when left alone one day, he had a feast—the carcasses of two Guinea fowl; six eggs plus shells; one tube of anchovy paste, including all the tube but the cap; and the bakelite caps and rubber nipples from three of the baby's bottles.

Ill effects? None. His bowels were slightly loose for a day, and his stools slightly green.

Dear Mr. Riddle:

I have never written to anyone on a newspaper before, but I just have to write to you. I have been reading your articles on feeding dogs, and I must say that you are absolutely crazy, as well as inhuman. Some dogs are really human beings but you are too stupid to know this.

We have four darling Chihuahuas, and they love to sleep with my husband and me. It is so cute to see them all curled up in the bed between us. We have the bed fixed up so they can get some air while under the covers.

Well, I get up first, and the dogs rush to their private bathroom, which is really the laundry room, while I perk the coffee. So then I take three cups of coffee into the bedroom, and the dogs rush back and get on the bed. Then we give each dog three teaspoonsful of coffee. They won't touch it unless it has plenty of cream and sugar in it. You see, they know they are human beings, but you aren't.

I hate you, Mr. Riddle

Positively,
Mrs. J. A. ⸻

NEWS NOTE

New York, N.Y.—Dogs are a major consumer of baby foods, a survey completed today, showed. Dogs consume about 46 percent of all canned milk production, and about 30 per cent of the formula type of baby foods. They are said to consume 20 per cent of baby canned vegetables.

But, on the other hand, consider this fact dredged up by a canned dog food manufacturer. During the depression years of the 'thirties' he surveyed his dog food sales market. He was startled to discover that about 20 per cent of his canned dog food sales was being bought for human consumption.

14

2

Dog Care and Training

STAY

Dear Mr. Riddle:

I need help with my Cocker Spaniel. He is the most wonderful dog in the world, and he is a perfect gentleman at all times. But he has one bad habit. He will bite anyone who puts his hand out to touch him, and particularly, babies. He has bitten three of them. And yet he has a truly wonderful disposition. How can I cure him?

Sincerely,
Joe _____

Release safety on .45 calibre pistol, place muzzle at dog's left ear, and pull trigger. The ironic part of this letter is that three months following its receipt, the owner of the dog was appointed to the Army war dog training corps.

Dear Mr. Riddle:

My sister died last year and left me her dog. It is a wonderful dog. But it has a bad habit, and unless you can help me, I am going to have to put this dog to sleep, even if my sister curses me in Heaven, which God forbid.

This dog is only a mongrel, and he is eight years old. But he was my sister's pet, and we love him for that. But I'm almost ashamed to tell you this bad habit that he has.

He sneaks upstairs and does his business in the middle of the bed spreads, or on the pillows. Is it because he misses my sister, or what? Is he too old to cure? Please help me before I do violence to my sister's memory.

Sincerely,
Miss _____

Dear sister in Heaven. Rest in peace. I cured the dog.

Dear Sir:

I have wire terror dog, and I heard they supposed to be smart. But this one sure dum. I think he completely crazy. I tried to train him but it just impossible. He eat cigarette butts and book matches. He love kids. But when he tied in back yard and see another dog, he go nuts and then he give a running leap at my back door and brakes the glass in my door.

As I have never took him to get any kind of needles do you think he got distemper? He is cute, name Patches. He play ball with my husband. But when my John bend over to pick up ball bite him in pants back side. Me when I bend over to pick up stick to hit him one bite me same place except under dress. Me and piles and this bite sure tough to sit down. You think it maybe rabies he got not distemper. You let me know.

I remain

Mrs. _____

Warning: Bend over only to pick up ball bat which, if used properly, will cure your cute dog of rabies and distemper.

Dear Kind Friend To Dogs:

Whenever we leave our dog alone, he tears down the curtains, dirties on the beds, and howls for fits. The neighbors get frantic. They have called police twice. Now someone has to stay in the house all the time. This is my son's dog, who is in Korea, so we can't shoot him, or otherwise dispose of him. Please help.

Sincerely,

J. H. _____

Send the dog to Korea, and let your son's captain do the worrying.

(This dog and the one in the previous letter, were cured by teaching them to sleep in an indoor kennel, which could be locked shut when necessary. The dogs gained a feeling of security and learned to stay in the kennels without complaint.)

Sir:

I am an elderly lady living alone with my dog. He is wonderful, but he just has fits when the telephone rings. This seems worse when he is tied outdoors. So I don't see how it can be the noise of the bell hurting his ears. I am on a party line. So when the neighbors hear my dog barking, they listen in on my conversations. This makes me mad. Can you help me?

Yours truly,
Miss‗‗‗‗‗‗‗

Private Eye Riddle investigated, and reports as follows:

When the woman put her dog outside, she tied him to the telephone ground wire. The dog had a chain collar, and the leash was made of chain links. The dog got shocked every time the phone rang. Just as Prof. Pavlov's dogs salivated when the bell rang, so her dog would have a barking fit, even when not shocked.

Dear Dog Editor:

I was told never to give a dog a bath. My puppy is a year old now, and he's beginning to smell a little. Is it true I can never give him a bath? He likes to lay in puddles and roll in nasty things. This smells up the place, and also the bed clothes, because he likes to lay in bed with us. Why can't he have a bath?

Sincerely,
Abner J‗‗‗‗‗‗‗

Don't give him a bath. Make an artificial puddle by filling a tub with water and put him in it. Play with him by rubbing him with soap. Wash out the soap with more artificial puddle.

If you play with your dog regularly in this way, he will forget to smell.

18

YES SIR, MR. RIDDLE, WE DOUSED HIM WITH WATER
LIKE YOU SAID . . . HE IS A REAL GOOD DOG
NOW . . . BY THE WAY DO YOU KNOW ANY ONE
WHO CAN PLASTER

Dear Mr. Riddle:

We have a dear little Boston Terrier who has been developing bad habits as he gets older. We can't go near him when he's eating. He has got so bad we've had to move his high chair away from the table.

He loves to ride in a car. But next he has taken to rushing out and jumping in first, and then we can't get in after him. If one of us tries to hold him until the other gets in, he bites.

And now he has got to staying in the bathroom, and we can't get in there, and we have to go to the neighbors to use the toilet. This has made my husband's constipation worse, and besides which, it is very embarrassing.

Yours Truly,

Mrs. A. F. _____

Dear Mrs. A. F . . . .

Do the things which usually cause him to growl or bite, and then dash water in his face. Wear heavy gloves while doing this and repeat the lesson four or five times daily. Have the water handy so that you can dash it in his face at any other time he growls or bites.

I would be interested in knowing the results.

Dear Friend:

Well, we tried your advice and it worked. We got some pails of water and went to the bathroom. And the minute he growled to keep us out, we threw the bucket of water on him. When we finished, the bathroom floor was three inches deep in water, and the downstairs plaster fell. But now he won't even go near the bathroom.

As you said to do, we tried feeding him from a pan on the kitchen floor, instead of in his high chair at the table. We sure used a lot of water. But as you predicted, we can now pick up his food dish while he is eating, and he won't even growl.

The water was hard on the car, too. But Junior hasn't growled or bitten for several days now. We can pick him up and pet him, and he's really more fun than he's been in years, thanks to you.

Still, we miss him at our mealtime. Do you think we can now let him return to his high chair, so that he can eat at the table with us?

Thankfully,
*Mrs. A. F*_____

Poor Junior. His fond owners won't let him be a dog. So it's a cinch, he'll return to his criminal ways.

Dear Sir:
My problem may seem funny to you, but I am nearly frantic. We have a wonderful Irish Setter, but he is bringing me to an early grave because of his one bad habit. He likes to lift his leg and squirt on ladies' legs. I have whipped him and everything, but it does no good. I have discovered that it's mostly with women wearing nylons that he does it.

Do you think he doesn't like women, or nylons, or women in nylons?

Anxiously awaiting your reply, and don't print my name.

Sincerely,
Mrs. Josie D.

Your dog must be descended from the famed Ch. The Baron Gore. He once caught the governor's lady across the ankles, and twice (indiscreetly) left his water mark on judges.

Dear Dog Man:
I have a dog which has been killing my chickens. Now I read where you should tie the dead chicken around his neck and let it rot there. And in this way, you could scold the dog right along, and he would get so sick of that chicken, he would never go near another.

So that is what I did. But the smell nearly drove us out of the house. And also, the house got so full of feathers, my wife got mad. Besides which, when the chicken got so rotten it fell off, Spotty quick ate the chicken, and even what feathers which were left.

So what do I do now?

Truly yours,
Frank W————————

Tie up your dog and eat the rest of the chickens before the dog does.

Dear Sir:

We have a dog and he is just wonderful. He is a Weimaraner, five month old, and he will heel perfectly, and sit where you tell him to.

He yelps and has a fit when I go to the basement. Yesterday I had to go away, so I locked him in the kitchen. But he broke loose.

He tore up the baby's crib, and tore out all the burners in our electric stove. He got one window kind of all soap like with his nose. The other window was open, and he tried to get through the Venetian blind, or maybe he wanted to tear it down. Anyway, he got hung up in it and vomited. A neighbor saw him and turned the hose on him. But he only tried to play in the water, as well as he could, being hung up.

We think he's wonderful except for this. And also, he howls when you leave him alone.

Sincerely,
Mrs.————————

What seems to be your problem?

GOOD NITE DEAR

I married a widower with a dog which is 10 years old. Now I like dogs, but this dog does not like me. In fact, I think it hates me. But my husband loves this dog.

What it does, which it also smells bad, is this. When it is time to go to bed at night, this dog rushes ahead to the bedroom. And then when I try to go in, it bites me. So my husband has to take the dog out while I get in bed. But then, in the daytime, it goes into the bedroom and won't even let me in to make the bed.

My husband thinks this is very funny. But it hurts when this dog bites me, even though he hasn't many teeth left. And also it scares me. What can I do about this? And also, as I said, it smells.

Sincerely,
Mrs. _____

This required a book length answer, but included the idea that the dog had lived a long and happy life, and maybe now it was time for him to go to dog heaven, via euthanasia.

Dear Dog Editor:

I wrote to you three years ago for help, and I am sorry I didn't take your advice. I am the woman who married a widower, whose dog bites me when I try to go into the bedroom. The dog is now 13 years old, but he is getting worse.

Now, he will not only not let me in bed with my husband, but if I get in before the dog gets into the bedroom, that dog jumps right up on the bed and tries to bite me, even when I hide under the covers.

Now I have to sleep on a couch downstairs, and my husband thinks this is very funny because he loves this dog. That dog, and he smells bad, sleeps under the covers with my husband. And what is worse, he has taken to sleeping on the couch in the daytime, and bites me if I go near that. What can I do about this?

Sincerely,
Mrs. _____

Such touching love between man and dog should be rewarded. Maybe it could be arranged for them to go to heaven together—and right now.

Reminiscence No. 1

A man owned an insane Coonhound, which was notoriously vicious. But he kept it because it was an incomparable cooner.

One day the dog killed his owner's three year old daughter. I was assigned to investigate and to write the story.

The details so horrified me, I wrote a dog column telling people how to teach their puppies that they cannot fight or bite under any circumstances. Now litter mates at six weeks old begin to growl and fight over their food. So that is when you begin the training.

My procedure, with my own Springer Spaniel puppies, was to hover over their community food dishes. At the first hint of a growl, a puppy would be grabbed by the tail, pulled backward, and then rolled over on the floor. Since puppies are so floppy anyway, they roll easily, and are not hurt. But a few lessons at the food dish teach them that they cannot growl or bite at anyone or anything.

With the older dogs, I have frequently used water, dashing half a pail of it into the dog's face. Or I have pelted the dog in the ribs with an empty tin can. This is most effective, since the dog doesn't understand this extension of your arm, which throwing the tin can represents.

I went into great detail on this, and in fact, to such an extent that only the first treatment—that for unweaned puppies—appeared in the first of two articles.

Now a doctor friend of mine had bought a 50 pound Springer Spaniel field trial dog in Canada. The dog had been guaranteed field trained, but nothing had been said about his disposition. He was vicious and untrustworthy.

The day after the first of these training articles appeared, I saw the doctor walking down the long city room of the old *Cleveland Press* building. His coat was draped like a cape over his shoulders.

The reason was quickly apparent. He had tried this training method on his dog. He had put down the food dish, then grabbed this 50 pound vicious dog by the tail, and had tried to heave him across the floor.

25

He was bandaged on the left side, from fingers to shoulder. And the moral of this tale is, I suppose, that many a good intention goes wrong.

Reminiscence No. 2

At the Cleveland winter sportsmen's show one winter, Cal Barry had a dog act. Among the dogs was a one-eyed Basset named Bruiser, and my own Springer Spaniel, Ryedale Anne. Bruiser was the clown of the act, and I was the "emcee."

I would tell the crowd that they would see some things they'd never seen done before, and some that were very funny. As to the former, it was true. Cal had the dogs retrieving live pheasants, ducks, rabbits, and pigeons, with a given dog being ordered to retrieve one or the other of the game animals. The dogs performed faultlessly.

They were all wonderfully obedient. All that is, except Bruiser, the Basset. As the clown of the act, he appeared to be untrained. He would wander about the stage, smelling here and there, and occasionally letting out a deep bay.

One night, Bruiser leisurely adjusted himself (hands on his knees, as they say in the dog game) and relieved himself in the middle of the stage. Cleveland Public Hall boomed with laughter from 20,000 spectators.

"Now Bruiser," I said over the speakers, when the crowd had quieted a bit, "you stop that sort of thing and act like a gentleman should."

Whereupon Bruiser, who had tape worms, and the rectal irritation which sometimes goes with it, rubbed his bottom half way across the stage.

That great auditorium almost collapsed with the noise and laughter. I was so surprised and embarrassed I forgot the routine, and got things out of order. But the crowd was laughing too hard to notice.

We had the dogs on display on benches in the exhibition hall under the main arena level. After our act was over, we took the dogs back to their benches. But during the early part of the show, a water pipe above the benching had burst, drenching the benches with rust so heavy it looked like blood.

Just as we reached the benches, the show's sign painter went by. So we had him paint a sign, which we hung up: "This is where we shot Bruiser, The Basset."

But the crowd, still hooting and roaring with laughter, came down after the show and nearly over-ran our benches. We were terribly embarrassed, and visioned ourselves getting fired. Instead, we found we were the heroes of an unforgettably funny incident.

And more than that!

A dozen people got me aside, and two dozen cornered Cal.

"How in the world did you teach Bruiser to do that?" they asked.

Reminiscence No. 3

Two years later, I had my own dog act at this same winter sportsmen's show. Two of my dogs had been in an accident, and I had borrowed two others. I had had only 18 days in which to train these dogs and to work them into the act.

One was a hard as nails hunting dog, a Spring Spaniel as rough and tough in the hunting fields as they come. But he had a bad habit, of which I knew nothing when I borrowed him. He had a hard mouth. Which is to say, he would crunch down on the game which he was retrieving.

I discovered this to my dismay when I placed a live pigeon for him to retrieve. I could not send him home because I desperately needed him in the act. So the only thing to do was to try to break him of his killing habits in the 17 days remaining.

I made sleeves of a tire inner tube, put roofing tacks through them, and then placed the pigeon in the sleeve. For several days, Blaze had to carry a pigeon occasionally, the while I warned him to be careful. If he crunched down, of course, he'd be pricked by the nails.

Next I would lead him up to a sleeved pigeon, make him sit in front of it, warn him vocally, and then have him pick up the bird. On the return, I'd walk beside him, while continually warning him.

After a time, I began to send him for the bird. But I'd stop him just as he reached it, warn him by voice, and then give the order to retrieve. He would obey. And a few days before the show, I found I could trust him to retrieve the pigeon unharmed even when there were no roofing tacks in the sleeve.

But I was astonished to notice something else. Blaze had become so used to stopping and sitting just as he reached the bird that he was doing it automatically. I did not know then that many of the great circus animal tricks are developed in the same way. That is, you see an animal doing something, and you just develop it into a trick.

So when the show opened, and it came Blaze's turn to perform, the "emcee" would state that dogs hated to pick up things encased in rubber. So here was Blaze, picking up a pigeon in a rubber sleeve, in spite of his dislike for it. No mention of the fact that I was afraid, as yet, to trust him with a pigeon outside a sleeve.

Blaze would gallop down the stage, stop and sit as close to the bird as possible while I raised my arm and blew the whistle to stop. Even his owner was amazed by this proof of training and control which I had over his dog.

However, Blaze had another fault as a field trial dog. Spaniels must sit and honor the flush and shot for the dog on the parallel course. Blaze would do this, but then he would begin to bark. And this is frowned upon in field trial circles.

Now my dogs had to chase live mallard ducks which were tossed into the artificial pool on the stage. The ducks would dive when the dogs approached. Sometimes, the dogs would catch the duck; others not. Anne, my own dog, was one who would dive under water after the ducks. And this made spectacular entertainment.

I had no faith in Blaze when in the water. If he caught the duck, he'd probably forget his hurried and all too brief period of training. In the excitement, he'd probably kill the duck. So the great old dog was made to sit at pool side while the others chased the duck.

Blaze hadn't been tested on this type of control. But, as it turned out, he stayed put during each of the 29 performances. But also, as was to be expected, he barked loudly and steadily every moment the dogs were in the water. The "emcee" was prepared for this, however.

"Blaze," he told the crowds at the start of the water work, "will be made to sit beside the tank and act as cheer leader. A truly marvelous training feat!"

"How in the world did you ever teach him to do that!" people would ask, after the show.

So now you know!

Reminiscence No. 4

Screen Actress Genevieve Tobin was one of the truly fine artists of the silent screen. Miss Tobin and Venita Varden (Mrs. Jack Oakie) were pioneer importers and breeders of West Highland White Terriers. And it was Miss Tobin who taught me the water cure for obstreperous barkers and fighters.

It happened this way.

We had seen and discussed all the Westies. And now we sat beside the swimming pool over iced drinks. On one side, the lawn came to the edge of the pool. And also close to the edge was a portable fence which penned in some three to four months old puppies.

"Why," I asked, "do you keep the puppies there beside the pool, for they are certainly ruining the grass at that spot."

"Well," came the reply. "Sometimes these Westie puppies can get into some serious arguments, I don't want them to grow up to be fighters. And neither do I want them to get all chewed up in the fights.

"So when a fight develops, I just reach over the fence, grab the puppies, and toss them into the pool. It breaks up the fight instantly. And moreover, after a few such dunkings there isn't a pup that will start an argument."

Miss Tobin also had a wooden platform under her bedroom window. When one of her dogs began to develop into a nuisance barker, she would set up a portable pen on the platform, and place the malefactor therein.

Each time the dog barked, someone would dump a pitcher of water out of the window and onto the dog. The dog would be quickly cured. I have used endless variations of this trick to cure hundreds of dogs with bad habits.

Now it is well known that dogs have different instinctive methods of fighting. Some dogs slash. Some rely upon quick, powerful bites, and dance in and out like boxers. Bull Terriers grab, hang on, and try to worry their jaws and teeth into a deeper, more punishing hold, without letting go of what they already have in their mouths.

On one occasion, I explained in detail Miss Tobin's method of stopping puppy fights to a Bull Terrier breeder. His eyes got a far away look, and for some time he considered the matter in silence.

"I don't know whether it would work with my Bull Terrier puppies," he said at last. "Or whether I'd be strong enough to make it work. When my puppies get into a fight, picking up one of them would be like trying to pick up a string of giant white sausages."

Dear Mr. Riddle:
   I owned a female West Highland White Terrier. Except for the following problem, she was a healthy dog. She had a very bad case of ticks. The problem was so severe we had to have our whole apartment exterminated. This was an expensive procedure. . . .

                    Sincerely,
                    Mrs. _____

At least you got rid of the apartment.

Dear Mr. Riddle:
   My dog is allergic to fleas, and even though I exterminate them, she just gets another batch. I love my dog, and I want to move somewhere where there are no fleas. Where is that?

                    Sincerely,
                    Mrs. _____

If you and your dog move North of the Arctic Circle, you'll be safe from fleas.

Dear Mr. Riddle:

I have a Dashound dog, and he is trained and wonderfully clean and quiet. A real gentleman, he is. But now I see where he has wee weed against all three sides of our gray sofa. And this has caused yellow marks that don't come out. So I took him down to the vet's and had him castorated. But it didn't do any good. . . .

Sincerely,

Mrs. _____

A real gentleman except (like the rest of us) when he isn't.

Dear Mr. Riddle:

My dog steals things, and he growls when I try to take things away from him. Once he hid behind the davenport, and when I reached back there, he bit me. How do I cure him of this? He's a real card this dog. It is so funny to watch him when I use my hair spray. He is afraid of it. Please help me because he is such a lovely dog otherwise.

Sincerely,

Miss _____

We told her to use the hair spray to get the dog to drop things, and also to punish him for growling at her. It worked. But then . . . See the following letters.

Dear Sir:

I read your article on using the hair spray in training my dog. Of all the nutty things! I tried it, and my dog jumped up in my face and sneezed. Right in my face. And it got my glasses all covered with glom. You better learn something about dogs before you write such stuff.

I'm mad at you.

Mrs. _____

Dear Sir:

I ought to send you a bill. You and your aerosol hair spray. I tried it on my Doberman Pinscher. It scared him so he backed up and smashed right through French door window. It cost me $12 to get him sewed up. And besides that, $18 for a new window glass. But I will say it causes the dog to react.

Sincerely,
Mrs. ⸺

Dear Mr. Riddle:

I have a black Pug dog, aged nine months. His name is Weiner, and he loves me very much. But he sneaks up in my room and has bowel movements on my bed, or beside it, just where I step when getting into bed.

He does this when I go away and leave him alone. I have heard that this is a proof of his love for me. But still it is very disgusting the way he shows it. And I hope you can tell me how to teach him to prove his love to me in some other way.

Yours truly,
Miss ⸺

Quit gallivanting around. Plan to stay at home nights. Or take Weiner along on your dates.

Dear Sir:

My dog problem is this. My dog runs away. And when I call him, he just runs the other way faster. Someone told me that when I call him, I should sit down on the ground. So I did. The first couple of times, I don't think he saw me. The next time he did. But then he came back and raised his leg and squirted on me.

Yours truly,
Miss ⸺

Maybe only another example of true love. The famous Irish Setter, Champion The Baron Gore, never saw me but he urinated against my leg. Fine way to treat a judge!

Dear Maxwell Riddle:

Apropos your column in the N.Y. Post on Spiteful dogs.

My wife and I inherited a wire-hair a couple of years ago. She was a delight and impeccable in behavior. But I have a small son from an earlier marriage, aged 7, and when he visits, the dog and he have no use for each other.

First time they met, the boy cased the situation and said to me: "Dad, how long do dogs live?" Maxie, the Wire-hair acted accordingly, and hid under her chair.

Over the holiday, the boy came for a visit. They seemed to be living in some kind of truce. Then I had to take the boy back to his home in Philadelphia. We left for Penn Station.

Maxie glowered as we went out the door. Then she glared at my wife. Then she stood in the middle of the living room, and deposited the biggest lump of business you've ever seen. And this was something she had never done in our experience. Boy, did she know what was going on!

Sincerely,

Jack _____

As well as I can discover, there are four dogs, six turtles, two toads, one lizard, three cats, and one salamander named after me. This Maxie is not!

Sir:

I have a standard Fox terrier who is just a doll and we love him. But I think he has a loose nut some place. He was born May the 15 of 64. We feed him a good meal 2 times a day and leave him a big bowl of Kibbles for inbetween meals. But he eats everything he put his teeth to. We have run out of things for him to sleep on rugs pillows old coats pants sweaters he eats everything. My husband has to help him some times the stuff gets caught in his rectum and he has to pull it out. He also is a good digger.

Can you give us some help on him we also feed him yeast tablets he weights 11 pounds and is as strong as a bull. Thank you for any help you can give us.

Mrs. _____

The theory of why dogs eat grass is, that since the grass is undigestible, all that roughage will scour out any worms the dog might have in his intestines. Lady, all I can say is, your dog shouldn't be afflicted with worms.

Dear Sir:

I have a two year old German Shepherd, and he is something of a problem. He eats everything in sight except human beings, whom he loves to death.

He has eaten six baby sweaters, half a dozen mittens, a couple of Gillette razor blades, some screws and nails, and even some of my wife's nylon hose, and one pair of her panties.

Now I know you field a lot of toughies. And I'm not going to ask you how to cure my dog, since I'm convinced he is completely insane.

All I want to know is, why doesn't this dog die from eating all that junk?

Sincerely,
Mr. _____

He's probably a bum in other ways too. Only the good die young.

Dear Sir:

I have a Collie that is one year and three months. We live in a third floor apartment, without elevator service, and I can't get my dog to go up or down stairs. She weighs about 60 pounds. I sure can't carry her anymore up or down stairs. Her nails are long and she won't let me clip them. She just gets wild and wants to bite me whenever she can. She still has to get her last shot, and I can't find a way to get her to the vet. Can you please help both of us?

Mrs. _____

You'll have to teach that dog "must" or strengthen you back and legs.

Dear Mr. Riddle:

I've got a French puddle. He keeps eating paper tissues. He actually swallows the paper, too. I've been watching his reliefs, and he seems to digest those tissues too. Can you tell

34

me why? Is it harmful to him? He seems to have a need to eat tissues.

Yours truly,
Mr._____

Possibly an internal cold?

Dear Sir:
I've got a male Boxer and he is awfully attached to our female cat. Recently she had six kittens. He cleans them up for her, and carries them all about the house. What would you say about that.

Sincerely,
"Anxious."

Crazy mixed up kid!

Dear Mr. Riddle:
I've got a female fox terrier, and she has the most astonishing thing. She is very jealous of our cat. Twice now, the cat has had kittens. Both times, Trixie has simply chased Vixen away and stolen her babies. She carries them to her own bed. And what is more, she actually develops milk and feeds them.
Is this good? The kittens seem to get along all right. But how can I be sure? We've taken the kittens back to their own mother, and Vixen has tried hiding them. But Trixie always finds them and steals them again.

Please advise me.
Mrs._____

Buy your dog her OWN cat.

Dear Mr. Maxwell:

Tank you for you advice in my last letter. Now we have a real trouble with our puppy. A family gave us a puppy 5 months old two months ago. We try to trainer she don't listen to us. She lick you hand then she bite you. She eat linoleum in the kitchen rug I must get after her, ouside she eat dry grass, wood, anything but nail or glass. What can we do with these dog, we love her Mr. Riddle. Another thing, she is always hungry we feed her four times a day large meal. Another important thing she can't bark she can't defend herself I don't know why she never bark, is anything we can do with her because if not we put her to sleep then she don't suffer. Nobody want a dog that don't bark. We appreciate it if you have any advice. So we can keep our puppy of 7 months. Is any hope?

Tank you very much. Very truly your

Mrs. _____

Here's a dog that can live off the land, or the house, and can't become a neighborhood barking nuisance, and you're complaining yet?

Dear Sir:

Some friends gave our son a puppy for Christmas two years ago. He is sort of mixed up, but he has a black snoot and ears, and looks like an Irish Terrier. He is such a sweet little thing, little but so loveable to my husband and myself. And best of all, he loves our son beyond anything. I just love himself beyond anything.

Our trouble is he wets around the house, even after being taken out. The doctor told us to lock him in the kitchen, but he only wets on all the chairs and the refrigerator. I wanted to have him casteriated, but the doctor said it wouldn't help. He has had all his shots, even for Rabbis. I'm at my wits end to know how to break him of this bad habbit.

I can't get rid of him. I love him too much. Do you have any new ideas?

Gratefully,
Mrs. _____

I have some. But you love him too much.

Dear Sir:

My dog is very high strung to the point of being positively silly. I cannot understand this. My wife and I are both Christian ministers, and we have tried to provide him with the best background. And we have given him the best possible music.

For instance, we have never let him hear jazz or rock and roll, but only the very finest recordings of symphonies and religious music. What do you think is the trouble?

I remain,

Very truly yours,
Rev. _____

Maybe boogey-woogey would wear him down.

Dear Mr. Riddle:

Thirteen years ago you helped us to train our dear little Welsh Corgi, Fluffy. We had her for 11 years until she died of old age and a stroke. Then we got this St. Bernard. She is now two years old. Is she too old for housebreaking and obedience training?

She is much too big to handle by force. If she messes in the house, we cannot even drag her back to show her and spank her for her sins.

I am getting very discouraged, but she is so overwhelmingly lovable that I cannot face getting rid of her. Is there any hope?

Hopefully yours,
Mrs. _____

Only human beings get too old to train.

Unusual Woman

A young lady of my acquaintance is a German Shepherd breeder, and an obedience trainer of note. Not too long ago, she had an argument with people who bet her that she could not control her dog, in public, by the use of signals alone.

My friend took up the wager, drove away, and shortly returned with her dog. It was early evening, but the area was one of stores, a delicatessen, and a bar. So there was a fairly constant flow of pedestrians.

The young lady worked the dog up and down the street using hand signals only. While she was doing so, a drunk staggered out of the bar. He leaned against a utility pole and watched the performance in obvious disbelief.

"My God," he said, "now I know I'm drunk. A silent woman!"

3

Odds and Ends on Dog Shows

IF SHE'S SO BAD, WHY DID YOU PUT HER BEST OF BREED?

Dog shows are a highly technical sport, both blighted and blessed by human, as well as animal frailties. If you keep your sense of humor, they're fun. If you insist that your dog win as a means of solving life's frustrations, then dog shows will give you ulcers.

Those who fatten life's entertainment by keeping dog shows a true sport, have a saying:

"You don't have to be crazy, but it helps."

Those who make steady winning a condition of staying in the game, invariably get out rather hurriedly. They, too, have a motto. It is:

"Dog shows are crooked."

But then, if it is crooked, the chances are they helped to make it so. They have become soured by life. And besides that, they have developed indigestion from swallowing, and from cursing the winning dog, which is invariably a bum.

Dog shows, like any other hobby, are expensive. Most breeders find that their hobby costs them four to five times what they get in return by selling puppies, grown stock, and stud services. Occasionally, someone who is smarter than the rest, or who gets into a breed just at the time it begins a tremendous popularity surge, does make money from dogs.

Which reminds me of a certain dentist friend of mine who went to dental school at the time when the Strongheart and Rin Tin Tin motion pictures were carrying the German Shepherd to world popularity heights. He decided to breed German Shepherds as a means of paying his way through school. Wherefore, he purchased a fine brood bitch.

As a term project, each man in the class had to make various types of filling in teeth, wire these to cards, and turn in the whole as a proof of his ability. My friend made up his card. But the night before the deadline for turning it in, the dog ate both the card and the teeth.

My friend had previously offered somewhat lame excuses for failure to be prepared. He was in the professor's dog house, and he realized that the old hard-shell was not likely to believe the term paper was being digested by a German Shepherd. So he took the dog to class as Exhibit A.

The professor lived up to expectations. He began a tongue lashing which, however, the student stopped when he offered the professor a bottle of castor oil. The castor oil worked during the examination period; the teeth were recovered and approved; and my friend is now a respected dentist in Knoxville, Tenn. And he's still raising dogs.

Not long after he told me this story, I got a call from a celebrated movie actress. She had visited a Weimaraner kennel in the Cleveland area, and had sat on the kennel floor to play with five half grown puppies. One of them scratched off a diamond ear ring valued at $2000. It promptly ate the ear ring.

"What will I do?" she wailed.

"Give it a dose of castor oil," I said, remembering the German Shepherd and the teeth.

"But how do I know which one to give it to?" she asked. "Those five pups are as alike as peas in a pod."

A veterinarian was called. Hearing the name of his client, he came on the double. All five puppies were purged, and the diamond ear ring was recovered.

Cuban dog fanciers supply a dark side to this situation. Many have been allowed to leave Cuba for the United States. But they have been forced to leave their dogs behind. Some have preferred to stay behind rather than to leave their dogs to an uncertain fate.

The reason the Castro government will not permit the animals to leave is this: It is afraid that the people will feed their valuables to their dogs, and then recover them in Florida as was done in the cases I have cited.

A breeder of purebred dogs can go almost anywhere in the world and meet people with similar interests. And sometimes dogs can grease the sled runners in unexpected ways. Consider my own experiences.

I was to judge at the Pretoria, South Africa, show a few years ago. Now South Africa is not partial to American newspaper writers. A special red tape procedure is set up, and visas are not granted automatically. For example, I was at first asked to swear that I would not write about South Africa upon my return to the United States. Eventually a visa was granted without this provision.

Upon arrival to Johannesburg, I was taken into the immigration office. The officer simply could not believe that an

41

American would be brought all the way to South Africa just to judge a dog show. Here was an admitted newspaperman making such a claim. The officer smelled something subversive about this. Questions were asked; time passed; things were getting sticky.

Then a goateed gentleman with a cane came up and spoke privately with the officer. Whereupon I was pushed over to the customs station with:

"Get along with you now. I've got a lot of people to see."

That's about the way it went with the customs officer. Did I have any American whiskey? No? Any jewelry? No? Any money to declare? No? Well, he would have to search my bags for himself.

The goateed gentleman spoke to him in private, stomping his cane lightly as he talked.

"All right. Close your bags and move on now," the officer said, not bothering to search them after all. "Move on now, I'm very busy."

The goateed gentleman was waiting for me outside the door.

"You don't remember me, do you?"

"Well, no. I'm sorry but I can't. You seem to have an English or South African accent. And I'm a long way from home."

"But I remember you," he said. "I'm the airport reporter here. I once worked for the Chicago Tribune, and I raised German Shepherds to help pay my way through the University of Chicago. You gave my German Shepherd best in show at Hammond, Indiana, in 1941."

Although I did not say so, I do not remember that I did award best in show to his dog. And I shudder still to think what might have happened had I put his dog down.

At Nairobi, Kenya, the kennel club turned out in toto to meet me at the airport. It was fortunate. I had a beautifully tanned springback hide, mounted on green velvet. It had been a gift of the Southern Africa Boxer Club.

"Where is your license to take this out of Africa?" the customs officer asked.

"I don't have a license," I replied. "I didn't know I had to have one. This was a gift to me, made at the Johannesburg Airport, and as you can see, the gift card is still on it."

"Yes, maybe so. But then where is your license to bring this skin into Kenya?"

"Well, again, I didn't know I had to have one. I . . . ."

"I'm sorry, but I'll have to confiscate this."

Whereupon a lady came forward to ascertain the trouble, which was then explained to her at length.

"Think nothing of it," she said to the officer. "I issue the licenses for Kenya. I'll make out both licenses for him in the morning."

She was a local Pekingese breeder, who came with the kennel club to greet me at the airport.

This, too, had its other side. I was to show color slides of dogs at a meeting of the Hong Kong Kennel Club. The meeting was to be at the small theater of the U.S. Information Agency. An American official was to supply the projector.

When told the identity of the speaker, he replied:

"Ah yes, I know the fellow. He only gave my Great Dane a fourth ribbon at San Francisco. You are welcome to the projector. But I won't be there to greet him."

De Luxe Carrier

On the whole, it seems that the most corpulent ladies have the smallest dogs. Thus, the super-bosomy babes are often seen with Chihuahuas. When the midget dogs are gaited about the ring by these ladies, it is always cause for amazement that the dogs are not squashed, like bugs under heel.

In Utah some years ago, there lived an oversized Brunnhilde who bred Chihuahuas. The late B. B. Berman, a noted vaudeville entertainer and Standard Schnauzer breeder, was judging. The big lady lifted her mite of a dog onto the table for Berman's inspection. Berman examined the dog.

"Lady," he said, "this class is for males, and your dog is a female."

She inspected her dog.

"So it is. I'm sorry," she said.

Whereupon, she bent over the table, lifted another Chihuahua from her bosom, and then placed the female where the male had been. Berman stood there, jaw hanging in astonishment.

"Sir, do you want to examine the dog, or shall I gait it first?"

Berman, the night club entertainer, recovered his poise with her first words. His jaw snapped into position.

"Lady," he said, "the rules say that you can't have an ineligible dog in the ring. That dog which you have in—in there" and he pointed to her bosom, "will have to be removed from, from the ring."

"It is not in the ring," she replied. "This is my carrier, and I always carry a dog there."

A Question Of Sex

At one of the great outdoor summer shows, the same dog got winners male and winners female. This happened in an entry of more than 100 Cocker Spaniels, in the days before the breed was split into varieties, according to color.

A professional handler came out of the ring carrying a black Cocker under his arm. A woman rushed up.

"What are you doing with my bitch?" she demanded.

"It's not your dog, and it's not a bitch," the handler replied. "It's a male, and I just got winners dog with him."

"It's mine, and it's a bitch," the woman answered in fury.

And she was right. The handler had grabbed the wrong dog off the bench, and neither he nor the judge had noticed. The woman then took the dog back into the ring. She won her class, and then got winners bitch. The handler then brought his male into the ring. It had not been shown before, and of course, had no right in the ring. But in the male classes, the handler had been wearing the correct arm band for the male. So the judge's book was properly marked. The bitch then beat the dog for best of winners. Apparently the eagle eyed "ringside judges," were no smarter than the real judge. They never learned of the deception.

This question of sex, or the lack of it, has brought up some wildly amusing, and somewhat ribald situations which have kept the dog shows rocked with laughter for years. They come up because of an American Kennel Club rule which says that male dogs must have two normal testicles, normally placed in the scrotum. A dog which has only one testicle descended into the scrotum is called a monorchid. One in which neither has descended is called a cryptorchid.

It is mandatory for the judge to disqualify either a monorchid or a cryptorchid. Quite often it causes great embarrassment for the judge, since more likely than not, the exhibitor will be a young girl or boy, or an elderly lady who is showing for the first time.

At an eastern show, one such dog was handled by a beaming elderly lady.

"Madam," the judge said, "I am going to have to call for a veterinary examination of your dog."

"Why, whatever for? Jodie is as healthy as can be."

"I suspect that he is a monorchid."

"A monorchid! Whatever is that?"

"Well, it means that the dog only has one testicle."

"I know. But ain't it a dandy?"

Another lady claimed that her dog had become emasculated in an accident. She waltzed merrily into the ring behind her dog, carrying the evidence in a jar with alcohol. Alas, the judge disqualified her dog anyway.

At a southern show, a judge once disqualified a Boston Terrier champion, writing in his judging book that it was a cryptorchid. It was a female. That judge has been barred from the show ring ever since.

At a midwest show, the writer offered to handle one of six dogs of a rare breed which a handler had brought to the show. The judge examined the dog, and then said he would have to call the veterinarian, since the dog was a cryptorchid. Since it was an outdoor show, the judge's words could be heard by the ringside.

There was nothing for it but to tell the judge that the dog was a female. The judge had forgotten that this was a class for males and females—an arrangement which is sometimes made for rare breeds.

The Dangerous Game

The writer judged at a Pacific Coast show some 15 years ago on a miserably hot day. The man in the next ring was six feet five inches tall, well proportioned. He was wearing a fancy vest and sports jacket, while the writer was in shirt sleeves.

"Why are you such a panty-waist? Why don't you take off that jacket and vest so you'll be more comfortable?"

"Mr. Riddle," was the reply, "you're from the East and you don't know California. I'm wearing a bullet-proof vest."

Those Classic Errors

Sometimes judges make errors which, because of their nature, become classics. That includes the writer, who will admit to his errors, or at any rate when they become classic in nature.

Beagles are divided into two height classifications. People speak of 13 Inch Beagles and 15 Inch Beagles. A Beagle is disqualified from the shows if he is over 15 inches at the shoulder. So the classes are "not over 13 inches, and over 13 inches but not over 15 inches."

It is only recently that judges have enforced the rule with consistency, having been nudged to do so by the American Kennel Club. But judges have always had the right, and even the duty, to enforce it.

I judged Beagles at a spring outdoor show, and did not call for a measurement of a single dog. Neither did any of the contestants, who also have that right. The following day, I agreed to serve as official measurer at another show. That judge demanded that all of the 15 Inch Beagles be measured.

So help me, I was forced to disqualify every one of those dogs for oversize. And I had judged every one of them the previous day.

Another classic boo-boo occurred at an Ohio show 25 years ago. The president of the club bred Samoyeds. A record American entry up to that time was drummed up—26 dogs. The show was a two day event, and Samoyeds were judged on the first day.

The following day, the judge was wandering along the benches before his morning assignment began, when he was accosted by a lady Samoyed exhibitor.

"We all enjoyed your judging," she began timidly. "But to tell you the truth, none of us knows what to look for in a Samoyed. You would be doing the breed a lot of good if you'd go along the benches and tell us the faults and good points of our dogs," she added.

The flattered judge agreed to do so. He twisted his handlebar mustache, stamped his cane, and assumed his most regal air. A crowd of Samoyed exhibitors gathered about. The judge walked silently along the benches for a time, and then picked out a dog to discuss.

"This little bitch represents about everything you don't want in a Sammie," he said. "She is too small. She has a weazel body. She hasn't any bone, and she's lop eared. She has an undershot mouth and . . ."

But the lady was pulling his sleeve.

"Judge," she whispered, horrified. "That's the dog you placed best of breed." It was the club president's dog.

One club foolishly decided to have a cocktail party during an intermission between the completion of the breed judging, and the start of breed eliminations for best in show. When the variety group judging began that night, the man who was to select best terrier could not be found.

The other five groups were judged while a search was made for the missing terrier judge. He was found to be quite drunk. A hurried committee meeting was held. Since the judge could stand up, it was decided to let him judge.

That group contained four best in show winning terriers and there were 12 terriers competing. The judge easily picked out these four, which he put behind him. Then, sensing that the pressure was off, he began to clown.

"I don't like this dog. Take it to the end of the line," he said loudly. "I just love that Irish Terrier," he said. "Move it up to second place."

He clowned in this way for 10 minutes or so. Then satisfied, he marked down four placings and passed out the ribbons and trophies. He had completely forgotten the four good dogs, which he had placed behind him.

Subversive

Police and Civilian Defense officials at Butler, Pa., once gave Wallace Larson, the noted professional handler, a severe grilling on the theory that he might be a Nazi. The incident occurred during the early war years on the night before the annual Butler dog show.

It came about in this way. Larson had left a Standard Poodle in his hotel room while he went out for a late supper. He had also left a light burning in his room. An air raid blackout test began while he was at supper. He, of course, had had no information that such a test was to be held.

So when the blackout began, the only violation in the entire city was in Room 604 of the hotel. Irate police and wardens rushed to the room. They had no intention of having that one room spoil a perfect test.

However, they were stopped at the door by the furious barking of the dog. The main hotel switch had to be thrown out of order to blacken that one room. This also stopped all the other electrical services in the hotel. When Larson returned, irate officers were waiting for him.

Judge's Errors

Once upon a time, there was a judge who admired everything English. Exhibitors used to say that, if you could just manage to let the judge know that your dog was imported from the United Kingdom, you could drag in a poor dog and win with it.

Now there was at this time a wonderfully proportioned Whippet named Flornell Glamorous. She was able to win many best in show awards. Also, she was always perfectly shown by a noted handler.

At a Western Pennsylvania show, our judge, the Anglomaniac, gave best in show to a Whippet shown by this handler. As is customary, newsmen asked him to state his reasons for giving the dog its high award.

"Why," he said, "that's the noted whippet, Ch. Flornell Glamorous. She was one of the greatest dogs in England, and she's had many best in show awards, both in England and in this country."

The only trouble was, Flornell Glamorous was not at the show. Little has been heard of the lesser dog since, and nothing of the judge. The American Kennel Club withdrew his judging license.

Dog shows are elimination contests. Breed entries are reduced through competition to a best of breed. These are reduced to six when variety group judging produces a best sporting dog, best hound, best terrier, best toy, best working dog, and best non-sporting dog. From these, a best in show is selected.

These higher honors, a group first, and best in show, are much coveted by exhibitors. Many have no hope of ever winning a best in show award, but do hope someday to win a variety group.

It is virtually inconceivable, therefore, that an exhibitor could file a complaint against a judge for giving his dog a group first. Yet such a case is reocrded in Canada. It came at a time when the English Setter, Champion Maro of Maridor, and the Smooth Fox Terrier, Ch. Nornay Saddler, were competing for a world record for best in show victories.

In this race which was being watched with passionate interest by the entire dog fancy, the owner of the terrier sprung a surprise. His dog, he said, had a foreign best in show victory.

To match this, the late Wilfrid Kennedy, took Maro of Maridor to Canada. Kennedy wanted Maro to become a Canadian champion as well as an American, and he hoped to get a couple of best in show victories as well.

Now Maro's favorite canine friend was an Irish Setter bitch of negative quality. In fact, Kennedy's handler felt it was beneath his dignity to handle her in the ring. Kennedy, however, wanted the dog along on the Canadian trip as a companion for Maro. So he entered both dogs in the Canadian show and agreed that he, himself, would exhibit the Irish Setter.

English Setters were judged in the morning. Maro of Maridor got fourth in his class. This created a sensation, but the judge did not learn about it until luncheon.

"Do you know what you did this morning?"

"No, not particularly. What?"

"You placed the world's greatest show winner, Maro of Maridor, fourth in a class of four."

The judge turned pale and appeared to be sick in the stomach. Pleading a sick headache, he left the table, went upstairs to his hotel room and went to bed. Entreaties by the show committee were in vain. He refused to return to the judging ring.

The committee told Kennedy of the situation, and asked him if he could think of anything. Kennedy took a bottle of Scotch and went to the judge's room. He poured drinks for the two of them.

"Forget what's happened," he said. "Maro has been defeated before. You used your best judgment. So that's that. The show needs you to finish your judging."

After several drinks, the judge dressed and returned to the show. But then, Kennedy had to show his Irish Setter bitch under this judge. The judge placed the dog best of breed and then made her best sporting dog. That's when Kennedy got mad and brought charges against him.

Judging Experience

Most show dogs are gentle. They have been taught to pose and to permit examination by the judge. Even so, a judge risks being bitten each time he enters the ring. He must be particularly careful with dogs entered in the novice class, since these are likely to be spoiled pets making their first appearance in the show ring.

The writer was judging at a western show when an elderly man brought a Great Dane into the ring. Both were obvious novices. As I approached the dog, it tried to bite me, and did succeed in making tooth marks as I jerked my hand away.

"I'm sorry," I said. "Your dog bit me, and I'll have to disqualify him."

"Oh, my dog is very gentle," was the reply. "He doesn't bite."

"I'm sorry, but he did snap at me, and here are the tooth marks on my hand to prove it."

"But he's really very gentle," the man insisted. "He

wouldn't bite anyone. Only when we arrived at the show this morning, the veterinarian thought he might be running a fever. So he put a thermometer in his rectum, and that scared him."

I had a most officious ring steward, and he had been listening to all this. Now he spoke up.

"Mister," he said, "that isn't the end that bit him. Now you get that dog out of here."

Madam And Her Dog

In the early days of commercial aviation in the United States, a Detroit woman entered her dog in an Ohio dog show. She came from Detroit by train, but she was returning by plane. So far as was known, she was the first dog show exhibitor to use air travel for her dog.

Reporters, including this one, were most excited about this. It made a good story, and it became a better one when the dog won best in show. Naturally, we filed a story to Detroit.

Now show dog people are proud of the fact that neither race, creed, color, or station in life disturbs the camaraderie of exhibitors. Day laborer and millionaire consort together. It's the dog that counts. The only thing asked of exhibitors is courtesy and good sportsmanship.

The Detroit woman was therefore accepted on her own terms—a breeder of fine dogs. However, she is possibly the only person to flare into anger when a judge addressed her as "Madam." The judge spoke unknowingly. But that is what she was, a Detroit madam, the operator of a house of ill fame.

By one of those wildly improbable coincidences, on this Sunday night when her dog was winning best in show, the Detroit police were raiding her house of ill fame. Of course, they found her not at home. So they welcomed our wire story.

When the plane, carrying woman and dog, arrived at Detroit, police as well as reporters were waiting for her.

Prudent City

No one who attended the Johnstown, Pa. show that Saturday will ever forget it. First, because it came on the day before Pearl Harbor. Second, because cautious city officials had had the toilet seats removed before the dog show moved into the building.

Horseman's Dog

At an outdoor show held in a football stadium, a famed professional handler brought a very large—and bumptious Irish Setter into the ring. When he took the lead off the dog preparatory to posing him, the dog bolted from the ring.

He leaped a ring fence and started to play with some Cocker Spaniels who were being judged in the next ring. They bolted.

The Irish Setter dodged a dozen people and ran up on the hillside back of the stands. The handler caught him and brought him back. Once more the dog bolted, leaped a ring fence, and got two Boxers into a battle in another ring.

He was brought back, and was shown without being taken off leash. The judge put the dog fourth and commented:

"Sorry this wasn't a steeplechase. If it had been I'd have had to give him first."

Sex Mixup

One of America's best known—and competent—professional judges was judging Poodles. He held up the ring for 10 minutes waiting for a noted handler. When the handler arrived, the judge had all the dogs move about the ring, then stopped them with this particular handler and his dog at the head of the line.

Judges are required to check all males for two testicles normally placed in the scrotum. He checked the dog, and after a moment, said to the handler:

"Well, he's got them, but they're awfully small?"

"Got what?" the handler asked.

"Testicles, of course," said the judge.

"But judge, she doesn't have any testicles. She's a bitch."

"Then what is she doing in open males?" asked the judge.

You guessed it, of course. The handler, in his rush, had simply snatched up the wrong dog. The ringside was somewhat mystified when he and his dog were sent out of the ring; were still more so when he brought the dog back, and she got winners bitch.

Dear Sir:

I love dogs. And so when you wrote about that coming show and what delightful entertainment it would be, I took you at your word. I went to that show. And I sat through it the whole day. And I've been sick ever since. And it is all because of your stupid carelessness.

I am bald, and I got my head real bad sunburned, and I have had to have hospital treatment. Hereafter, you should warn people. And since maybe they won't read your warning, you should hold dog shows inside or under tents. I don't want no one to go through what I've been through.

Sincerely (mad)
Mr. _____

The Ravenna dog show supplies all judging rings with sun tan lotion. But exhibitors and spectators are on their own.

Isolating the Judge

I checked into a motel in a southern town. The motel operator said he knew who I was, and that he was going to put me in the farthest away room upstairs at the back of the motel where no one could get to me. I didn't complain. But as I was leaving the lobby, he said:

"Oh, by the way, I'll be showing Wirehairs under you tomorrow."

With better dogs, he might have won.

4

Why People Dislike Dogs

and Dog Owners

WE HELD HIM A LOT WHEN HE WAS JUST A PUP.

As a group, dog owners are not more inconsiderate than are other people. Neither are they more vulgar, more untidy, or less clean. But those who are below the average can certainly get all the rest into trouble with non-doggers.

A very pretty young woman came to me one time for advice concerning a dog she wanted to buy. This girl wanted a book full of knowledge off the cuff, so to speak. And I obliged by answers to the point.

"Gee," she said finally, "dog owners certainly have to learn the facts of life in a hurry."

And it is true, they do have to learn them. One of the really marvelous things about the dog fancy is to see youngsters discussing, without self consciousness, the specific details of mating and birth problems.

It follows from this that dog fanciers have slightly different standards than other folks. They can laugh and joke about matters which, to others, are vulgar and lacking in taste. But they can be as innately and actually proper as can any other group of people.

Clevelanders were, for example, thoroughly horrified by an incident which occurred in the lobby of the Statler-Hilton Hotel. Indeed, the two women involved were highly embarrassed. But the dog fraternity rocked with laughter for weeks.

A lady had flown in from the Pacific Coast to have her female mated to a dog which I owned in partnership with another woman. I kept this male in my kennels, 38 miles from Cleveland. My partner met lady and dog, checked the lady into the hotel, and then drove the woman and her dog to my kennels.

But attempts to mate the two dogs were useless. The female fought off the male. Finally, my partner suggested that she take the male back to Cleveland, so that another attempt could be made the next day, but without driving the long distance to my kennels. This was agreed upon.

The two women drove directly back to the hotel. And because the Californian wanted an additional chance to study the conformation of the male, she invited my partner and dog to her room.

It was 5 p.m., which is among the busiest periods for ho-

tel elevators. So the two women and their dogs had to wait for an elevator in the crowded lobby. They talked animatedly, and it was not until horrified hotel guests began to murmur that they realized what had happened.

The two dogs had decided between themselves that this was the proper time to mate. The dogs were dragged onto an elevator which arrived; no other guests were allowed to board; and the two thoroughly embarrassed women were given an express ride to their floor.

When we made out the registration papers, my partner asked in apparent innocence:

"It says here 'time and place of mating'." Do you think I dare say: Lobby of Hotel Statler Hilton, 5 p.m.?" We did this with giggles, and to the immense enjoyment of all in the dog fraternity who heard the story.

We mentioned above, the young lady who said that dog owners certainly learned the facts of life in a hurry. Is this wrong? It seems inconceivable to anyone with dogs that a 28 year old man would not have even a rudimentary knowledge of animal mating. Yet consider.

A 28 year old colleague on the Cleveland Press, who has a master's degree in education, came to me privately.

"Today I saw the most peculiar thing," he said. "I saw two dogs which seemed to be joined together at their rear ends. Is it possible that there are Siamese twin dogs?"

I explained things to him, including in my explanation why cats howl so during mating. I discovered later that he thought I was kidding him. The moral of this is that more people should own pets, else the race is in danger of dying in simple ignorance.

Now, I am in sympathy with the outrage of the manager of the Statler Hilton Hotel. But what happened in his lobby was an accident, and so no one could be truly blamed. I am not in sympathy with those who lack normal consideration for the feelings of others.

The following incident happened in a small Indiana city on the Erie Railroad. It was Mothers Day. I got off the train at 6:30 a.m., for I was judging the dog show in that city on that day. A man whom I knew slightly got off another car, and went to the baggage car to get his Doberman Pinscher.

There was only one cab, and I suggested that we share it. He agreed. I was not judging Doberman Pinschers, so there could be no scandal resulting from sharing the cab. We would go to the hotel and have breakfast together, then could go separately to the show later.

The man got his dog, and I supposed we could go directly to the hotel. But no. The man had other ideas.

"Driver," he said, "Take us to the nearest cemetery."

And then, turning to me:

"I always go to a cemetery first. They are usually fenced. There are plenty of trees and tomb stones. So it makes a perfect place to exercise my dog. He can get some running, and can clean himself out. And yet there is little danger of losing him."

Dozens of people were already in that cemetery decorating graves with floral displays. I sat there in horror, and absolute disgust, as the dog was let out of the cab. We were not harmed by those in the cemetery. But I could not have blamed them had we been mobbed. And I'm certain dogdom made some bitter enemies that morning.

Several of us went, one evening, to the 14th floor of a fashionable Detroit hotel. We went to visit a famous professional handler, and one of the greatest English Setters of his time.

Because of the dog's great value, the handler had instructions never to leave the dog at a show. Consequently, the handler always took the dog with him to his hotel room. We spent several hours talking and then, since it was after midnight, decided to leave.

"I think I'll go to bed too," the handler said.

"Aren't you going to take the dog outside for exercise, first?" he was asked.

"Oh no," was the answer. "As soon as you get on the elevator, I'll turn him loose in the corridor. He'll clean himself out."

A hotel once advertised that it accepted dogs because:

No dog smokes cigarettes in bed, and burns up the blankets.

No dog steals towels (even if its owner does).

No dog goes off to a show and leaves every light on.

No dog spills liquor on the beds, breaks the furniture, or goes to bed with its shoes on.

No dog sneaks out without paying its bill.

"Yes," said a hotel manager in rebuttal. "But plenty of dog owners allow their dogs to bring infestations of fleas into hotel rooms. Plenty of them let their dogs soil the rug, and chew on the chair legs. Plenty of them give their dogs baths in hotel tubs, and clog the drains with hair. And plenty of dogs bark and howl for hours when they are shut up in rooms while their owners are out on the town."

And the only answer that can be made to that one is: It depends upon the owner.

Depending upon your point of view, the best or worst advertising for a dog show is the trail of dog stools from hotel to show building.

Mindful of such publicity, the Western Reserve Kennel Club of Cleveland once hired what is euphemistically called a "sanitary engineer," to keep the sidewalk approaches to the dog show clean.

But as can be imagined, such an unwarranted expenditure of club funds was not approved a second year.

Dear Sir:

We have a Basset hound dog, a male, about two years old. He's apparently house broken. But the other night, we had some friends in to call. And after they left, the dog wet on the rug right where the woman had been sitting on the sofa.

He did the same thing when my grandson came one day. They have a horse and burro at their place, and I thought maybe he could smell the odor from the horse and burro.

Now I'm afraid to let him in after we've had company. What can I do?

Sincerely,
Mrs. _____

This is a switch, eh? A dog that doesn't like people guests!

Dear Dog Man:

We have a Begal dog which we love very much. He is just wonderful, but he has one bad habit. He does insist upon going over onto the nabor's porch to do his bisness.

I don't see why the nabor gets so mad. Especially when I am willing to clean it up. Can't you tell that nabor to be reasonable? What can I do?

Yours, trulee,

Mrs. _____.

Give the dog to your neighbor. Then maybe it will relieve itself on your porch, and the problem will be solved.

Dear Mr. Riddell:

My neighbor has a dog which is a bad barker. He ties the dog on a chain and stake on account of the leash law here. But our houses are close. I am a widow and I work a night shift. And in the daytime when I want to sleep, there is that dirty dog right under my bedroom window barking his head off.

I read where you said a man could stop his dog from barking by turning the hose on him. So I ran my hose into the bedroom, and when he got to barking I turned the hose on him.

This worked fine, but then the neighbor got mad. He got his hose and then sprayed my kitchen, right through the screen door, and soaked everything.

I don't want trouble, but what can I do?

Sincerely,

Mrs. _____

Lady, you've got trouble. Go to court and pray the judge is a reincarnation of Solomon.

Dear Animal Writer:

I have a darling little mixed breed dog. On account of the leash laws, I take it for a walk on leash. I always like to go one block west, because there is a park area there, and my little Tweaky and I like to listen to the birds.

But there is a meaney about four doors down. His dog is a bad fighter. Every time I go that way, even if on the other side of the street, he lets that dog out and it attacks mine.

So I took a good heavy cane along last time. And when the dog came rushing at mine, I batted him over the head. Then the man rushed out and called me filthy names. What can I do?

Sincerely,
Mrs. ——————

Wear ear plugs and carry a baseball bat.

5

Dog Fighting

Some dogs enjoy fighting and others fight from jealousy or boredom. So dog fights are common in kennels. Other dogs can be made to fight at will. Almost any man will brag when his dog has won a fight. It is not strange, therefore, that dog fighting is still an organized, if under cover, activity in the United States. The fighting dogs are called American Pit Bull Terriers by the United Kennel Club, which registers them. When registered by the American Kennel Club, they are called Staffordshire Terriers. Dog fights, being illegal, are advertised as "conventions."

I know a man who is opposed to dog and prize fights, but who is an ardent cock fight fancier. He has, at times, raised fighting chickens. I once asked him how he could square these apparently opposing attitudes.

He flew into a violent rage.

"Damn it," he said. "A dog is a human being. But a chicken doesn't know anything. He can't even feel pain."

In a magazine devoted primarily to dog fighting, I once saw a startling advertisement. Here it is, with the names changed.

"Joe Sloppo has piloted his dog, Sir James, to a bench championship as a Staffordshire Terrier. Now he is looking for a pit championship. We hereby challenge Joe to produce his dog in a pit at any weight, at any time, and for any amount of money he wants to bet.

"Our dogs have never been known to eat the face off a man, drunk or sober, but they have been known to take hold of a dog in a pit."

One must assume, from this, that Joe Sloppo's dog had bitten a drunkard in the face. At least, this is a charitable way to look at it. As for the dog fight, it never came off. The following advertisement appeared the next month.

"I've tried for years to get a fight for my Sir James, and none of you guys would produce a dog in the pit. Or anyway, not until Sir James started to get old. Now I'm in the Navy fighting the Germans, and I'm too busy, and you guys know it."

The same magazine once published a letter which read as follows:

Dear Sir:

I heard tell that Pete Reilly raises the best fighting dogs

in the world. So I wrote to him, and bought one of his dogs. When the pup arrived I was mighty disappointed in his looks, and I wrote Reilly and said so.

But he wrote back and said: "Don't you feel bad about that pup. His sire and dam were dead game in the pit, and he will be too. You just let him grow up and you'll see I'm right about him."

Well, on the fourth of July my Bozo, now 13 months old, got out and went hunting for dog meat. Before we could catch him, he killed two dogs and put three more in the hospital.

It cost me $50 doctor bills for those dogs. So I'm here to tell one and all that Pete Reilly raises the finest dogs in the world. And I would never hesitate to recommend him to anyone wanting a real good one.

Sincerely,
Jerry S —————

But would anyone recommend Bozo or his owner to anyone but the riot squad?

Dear Mr. Riddle:

It is true that I live in Pakistan, and maybe you will not want to help a man living so far away, because your paper is not sold in my country. But I read about you in Time Magazine, and I need your help.

I have an Alsatian dog and he is very gentle at all times. My neighbor has his brother. Now my neighbor and I are good friends, and we like to walk our dogs together. But when they meet, these two dogs fight. And I think that this is going to ruin a good friendship, because we both want to walk our dogs at the same time. So what do you recommend?

Sincerely,
Mohammed S.J.

The possibilities are infinite, and dazzling.
1. *Let the dogs fight until one is dead, or until one surrenders.*
2. *Walk in opposite directions.*
3. *Make both dogs wear muzzles.*
4. *Ship one dog to Peiping and the other to Moscow, and buy yourself some goldfish.*

Dear Dog Editor:

There is a man down the street which has a bad, mean Boxer dog which has beat up all the dogs on this street, and several others besides. And this man brags about his bad dog.

Now I do not own a dog. But I do not like this man for his bad dog, nor him either. And I want to buy me a real mean Guaranteed fighting dog that will clean up on this bad dog.

Money is no object with me, because like they say in church, this is for a good cause. I am willing to go as high as $3. Only I don't want to get gypped. I want a real trained fighter and Guaranteed. So you tell me where I can find him.

Sincereiy,
Mr. A. B _____

Sorry, old man. The real mean, trained fighting dogs cost at least $4, and the guaranteed one, $5.

Dear Mr. Riddle:

I know you write about the zoo too. Now I have a dog and a cat. But I am an animal lover from way back when. And I want to get me a tiger kitten which I can raise to be a pal to my dog and cat, and also for a playmate for my children.

I have heard tell that the zoo tigers do not nurse their kittens. So you fix it up for me. When there is a litter borned at the zoo, I will raise them all on bottles, and then I get to keep one.

I think my kids will be the envy of the whole city, walking that tiger around. But I worry though that dog and cat will not accept the tiger as a friend. So you fix me up.

Sincerely,
Joe S _____

I'm not worried at all about that dog-cat-tiger relationship, Joe. If you keep that tiger stuffed with enough children, he won't bother your dog and cat, and I'm certain they won't bother him.

Dear Mr. Riddle:

I most urgently need your help.

I have a lovely, sweet dispositioned tom cat. Only in so far as dogs are concerned he is an absolute devil. He hates them. And he has terrorized every dog in the neighborhood.

Only yesterday he went a block down the street, and then a block to the left, and he climbed over a fence just to attack a nice little dog which was minding her own business in a fenced in yard. And what is more, he bit the dog's poor owner in the foot when he tried to rescue his dog.

Can you help me?

Sincerely,

Mrs. —————————

Dear Neighborhood Dogs: Fear no more. At our suggestion the lady built an observation platform for her cat, and then put him on a rope.

Dear Dog Editor:

My six months old male puppy was attacked by a big dog. My dog was bitten in a most tender spot, which you will have to guess, since I am ashamed to mention it.

Now this is a valuable dog, and I bought him so I could sell stud services later and send my kids to school. What I want to know, Mr. Riddle, is will this make him shy away from sex. Because if it will, I am going to sue the owner of that big male?

Sincerely,

Mrs. —————————

Only time, and female dogs in heat, will tell.

Dear Editor:

I have two of the cutest little girl dogs you ever saw. But they get into terrible fights. And this is not right. Girl dogs are not supposed to fight. Boy dogs, yes, but not girl dogs. Do you think it is possible these girl dogs are over-sexed? Could they be both sexes at once, like I've heard about?

Now I was thinking to have some puppies from these dogs. But if they are all mixed up in the sexes, then maybe I'd better not, don't you think? Or could I be feeding them wrong?

Sincerely,
Mrs. _____

Imagine a married woman who hasn't yet learned that the female is deadlier than the male!

Dear Mr. Riddle:

I got a mean dog. He wants to fight all the dogs in the neighborhood, and he even bites the kids. Not me, because I let him have one with a ball bat. Now what I want to know is I heard that meat makes a dog mean, and so I ain't giving him none.

But that pup was mean when we got him. And it seems like to me that he is getting meaner since we ain't giving him no more meat. So I want to know if this what I heard about meat is true. And if it ain't what do I feed him to make him sweet like other dogs?

Sincerely,
Mr. _____

Have you tried feeding him honey and soft soap?

6

Dog Writers Know Everything

SAY MAX, YOU WRITE A DOG COLUMN AND KNOW ALL
ABOUT DOG PROBLEMS, WELL I HAVE A REAL PROB-
LEM, MY PET TURTLE . . .

There is no reason to suppose that because a dog man writes about dogs, he therefore wrote the biology text book, and is a naturalist as well. But, if there is much illogic in such an idea, it is nevertheless shared by millions of people.

After my dog column had established itself in the Cleveland Press, I began to get hundreds of letters and calls which did not concern dogs at all. The fact that the switchboard operators shared the same views as the public did not help.

The calls would go like this:

"There's a queer looking bird in my back yard . . . " "I didn't know who to call, and since you write about dogs, I thought maybe you could tell me how many days it takes a robin's egg to hatch." "Since you know about dogs, maybe you can tell me what is wrong with my parakeets . . . "

You, dear readers, will know one of the answers, at least. I had to learn about wild life, cats, monkeys, canaries and parakeets, and tropical fish. But, to learn about them, you have to own them. And so my home became a zoo of sorts. Of course, you can't do much about owning wildlife, except as you keep pet skunks, various snakes, and raise orphans of the animal world. And this I had to do.

A number of incidents involving the "you know this, so you must know that" psychology, stand out in my mind.

A new columnist had been hired by the Cleveland Press. He was a tall, elderly minister, who was to write a religion column.

Charles Schneider, who was then head of the Public Service Bureau, and is now editor of the Memphis Press-Scimitar, stood at the front of the city room pointing out the writers. I saw him point to me, and as he did so, the new columnist headed my way.

Gordon Meek, the labor editor, sat next to me.

"So, he is coming to ask me an animal question. And I will bet you it is not about dogs," I said.

"No bets," was the reply. "I've heard and read those crazy questions you get."

"So you're the dog editor," said the new columnist, after

he had introduced himself. "Since you know about dogs, I thought maybe you could enlighten me on a most fascinating subject.

"My children have just descovered a huge caterpillar, and they have had the great fun of watching it spin a cocoon. But you see, we haven't the slightest idea as to the identity of this caterpillar. And I thought possibly you could identify it for us. It would make the whole thing so much more fun," he asked.

I asked him for a description of the caterpillar, but he had not thought to look at it closely. So I gave him some leading questions, as the lawyers say. Then I gave him the answer.

"That is the bombyx mori, the American silk worm," I told him. "It produces good quality silk, but the trouble is, it spins the thread in such a way that it can't be unwound."

The new columnist went away mightily pleased. Gordon Meek, my neighbor, was pleased, too.

"You're a faker," he said. "You let him think that you're a regular encyclopedia of the animal world, whereas the truth is, you just accidentally happened to know the answer."

Gordon was right, of course. The United States had just placed an embargo against Japanese goods in those months before Pearl Harbor. The city editor, in consequence, had had me write a section page feature on how the embargo would affect the American people. So I had been researching the silk industry, and knew about the family of the bombycids.

But Gordon had missed the point. The new columnist had gone away convinced that his logic was correct, and that I knew no more than a dog writer should.

This same columnist once called me about his cat.

"She's acting most peculiarly," he said. "She sort of scootches down in front, shoves up her hind end, waves her tail, and gives forth the most plaintive cries.

"Now my wife felt that she must be quite sick, and the children are very upset. But I figured that she was lonely, and needed to get out into the fresh air. Probably wanted to prowl about as cats do, you know.

"This upset my wife further. But I told her she'd probably come back well satisfied and content. Don't you think I'm right?

"Yes," I replied. "She'll come home satisfied, and also pregnant."

Another such instance of dog writers knowing everything occurred on the Pennsylvania Railroad's New York to Cleveland train, the Clevelander. It stopped at Ravenna to pick up Cleveland commuters, which included me.

The conductor came rushing through the train, calling for a doctor. There was no response, no doctor being aboard. The conductor spotted me.

"A man has just cut his throat in the washroom," he said.

"But I'm not a doctor."

"No, but you're a dog man, and you know how to handle such things."

Well, of course, there was the time on the Arizona desert when I had to sew up a horse with ukelele string. And the time when the Labrador, Timmie, nearly cut off one hind leg, and I held the edges of the artery together until we got to the veterinarian. So I went along with the conductor.

The man was lying on his back unconscious. Blood spurted from his neck. Steam rose from the hot blood which soaked his clothes. I did the best I could to hold the cut artery together until a doctor and an ambulance arrived.

I don't know whether or not my efforts saved the man's life. But the man thought they had. When I went to see him at the hospital, a couple of days later, he cursed me for it.

Then there was the lady who called on the phone.

"I know you know all about dogs. So maybe you can tell me what makes my parakeet have an affinity."

"An affinity for what?

"For my red nail lacquer.

"Well, what do you mean an affinity for it? Does he try to bite your finger nail? Or does he try to peel off the lacquer?

"No, you don't seem to catch on so good. When he sees that red lacquer, he flies onto my finger and then, well, speaking frankly, he goes through the motions."

"You mean he makes mating motions?"

"Yes, that's it. It actually seems like he's trying to make me."

"When the bird is in his cage, does he spit up his food and put it in piles before a toy or mirror?"

"That's just what he does. But how did you know that?

"I guessed it. Sometimes parakeets appear to have abnormal hormone production, or at least an imbalance, and then the males will court toys by making food presents to them."

So she was happy, that girl.

"I knew that you, being the dog editor, would have the answers," she said in hanging up.

Several years ago, I had an exchange of correspondence with a man who had a parrot problem. His two letters follow.

Dear Sir:

This is not about dogs, but about our parrot I got for my wife for her wedding anniversary. This is a fine parrot, and it has many interesting habits, although my wife doesn't much agree with me on this. When someone is leaving the house, but not all the time, it says: "Goodbye, you son of a b_____"

He said this the other day when the minister was leaving, and I like to died laughing, because I kind of feel the same way, except not in such strong language. I'm not religious. This made my wife mad because she doesn't think this is so funny that I laughed.

And now my wife thinks I got that parrot trained to say that, thinking she might take the hint, too. This is not funny for me either. Because now she says if I didn't teach it to say that, prove it. And I can do this by teaching it not to say that.

That's where you came in. You've got some cute tricks with those dogs. So you cure my parrot of saying that, and I will buy you a case of dog food.

Sincerely,
L.V. _____

Dear Mr. Riddle:

Now I done just what you told me with that parrot, and I sure cured him in a hurry. But I don't think you are so smart either.

I got half a dozen glasses of water and set them about the way you said, in handy throwing distance. But that parrot doesn't say that everytime someone leaves. So I had to waste three days waiting for him.

But when he said it, I get her good, too. I near died laughing, but she threw two books at me. She claims I done it on purpose, and she can't understand that I couldn't hold off just because of her. I might have had to wait three days more.

Well, I caught him good a second time, and so now he don't say that any more. But here is where I don't think you are so smart. Now he won't talk at all. I know you said you couldn't accept the case of dog food . Well, don't worry. I ain't going to send it to you. Not unless you teach that parrot to talk again.

Yours truly,

L.V. _____

I'm not talking either.

Dear Sir:

You write about dogs, and so I know you can help me with my problem.

My son, who will be nine years old next month, has a passion for snakes. He catches them out in the fields and brings them home in jars and boxes.

This is bad enough for a boy. He thinks that because I'm his mother, I've got to like snakes, too. Well, I don't. And besides which, this is an unnatural passion. The Bible says so. It says a man is supposed to step on a snake's head, because it gave Adam the apple.

Now this is last straw. I started to clean out my boy's pockets last night after he went to bed, and I stuck my hand right into a cold, slimey, wriggling, live snake. I still have goose flesh thinking about it even today.

Even if you don't know how to cure my boy of loving snakes, maybe you know where the story of Adam and the apple and the snake appears in the Bible. I could at least read him that story.

Sincerely,

Mrs. _____

"In the beginning, ... "

7

Field Trials

When a new sporting dog comes onto the scene, the people who take up the breed are usually novices. Or, they are sportsmen who failed in their efforts to train the dogs of other breeds which they've had. The new breed is just automatically the world's best sporting dog, and it really doesn't need any training at all. Or, so they've been told.

The novices who take up the new breed don't know anything about training dogs in the first place. Many have had little shooting experience of any kind. Perhaps they can read, but it doesn't occur to them to search out a book on dog training. And for this breed, there may be no such book.

The newly baptized sportsmen discover quickly enough that every dog has to be trained; that each dog presents individual problems; and that the new breed is no better and no worse than any other breed, although it may be better suited for the kind of game in that hunting area than some other breed.

These newcomers to dogdom solve their training problems, or don't solve them, with the wildest kind of tricks, gadgets, and gimmicks. They stumble along as best they can, pooling what little knowledge they have with their fellow newcomers. It is an axiom that they ruin two or three dogs before they get the knack of proper training.

This was the case 30 years ago when the English Springer Spaniel became popular as a field dog in Ohio, and Western Pennsylvania, and in the Detroit area of Michigan. The Springer was supposed to be, and many consider that he is, the world's best pheasant odg.

Those sportsmen who had failed with Pointers and Setters turned gladly to the Springer Spaniel. They hadn't been successful in teaching their dogs to hold a point. Well, here was a dog which didn't point. So you were already on top of the game. Or so they thought.

The Springer Spaniel is supposed to hunt with a man on foot. It is supposed to hunt the area in front of the slowly walking hunter, flushing fur or feather—rabbits or pheasants, partridge, and quail—for the hunter's gun. To do this, the Springer has to stay within gun range of 30 to 40 yards.

Now, of course, there are liars who claim they can consistently knock down pheasants at 50 to 60 yards. But the average shooter has a range of accuracy not greater than 40 yards.

So it follows that any dog which flushes game at a range of more than 40 yards from the shooter is worse than useless. He's helping the game not his owner. And he is pushing his owner toward a massive apoplectic attack as well. And that's the problem with the Springer Spaniel—keeping it within gun range.

Now at Springer and Cocker Spaniel field trials, two dogs work on parallel courses. They must not cross onto the other dog's course; they must sit when they have flushed the pheasant; and they must not go out to retrieve until ordered to do so. This is called dropping, or being steady, to flush and shot.

The sportsmen who failed to train their Pointers to hold a point, now discovered that they had just as great a problem in teaching a spaniel to stay within gun range, and to drop to flush and shot.

The writer judged one of the very early Pennsylvania trials, near Newcastle. One dog would flush the pheasant and then chase it about 30 yards. Meantime, the handler would be blowing his whistle—an instrument designed to save the handler's larnyx from breaking under the strain. Or he'd be yelling "hup," which is the traditional vocal order to "sit."

Each time, the dog would refuse to drop to flush. Each time, he'd chase that 30 yards or so, and then, when the handler had given up, he'd sit. It was a puzzling performance, and after the trial I asked the owner for an explanation.

'I don't know for sure," he said. "But I've been banging him in the ribs with an air gun when he chased. However, I don't like to use the air gun when he is too close to me. I'm afraid I might do more than just 'sting' him. So I guess old 'Shot' has just learned how far out he can go without getting shot."

The Perfect Dog

A man showed up at one of our early group training sessions with his Springer Spaniel. We welcomed him, and invited him to join the club, and our training classes.

76

"Why should I?" he asked. "My dog is perfect already."

Still, he stayed about all day, watching the training. And when we had our next session, which was an informal trial, he entered his dog. His perfect dog wouldn't stay within gun range, couldn't be kept on its own course, and refused both whistle and voice commands to drop to flush and shot. So the man rather sheepishly asked us how we got such control over our dogs. We thought we'd pull his leg a little.

"Joe here uses a rock. He used to be a Big League pitcher. So he lets his dog get so far out, and then he bangs him in the ribs with a rock. That makes the dog think he can never get out of reach or control.

"Pete uses a sling shot. He can really smack a dog in the ribs at 25 yards, though he did put one dog's eye out.

"But Frank uses an air rifle—one of those kind which pumps to any desired pressure. He gets the pressure strong enough to sting, but not sufficient to penetrate."

This latter was, of course, true, although Frank had done this only once. But hearing this, the man with the perfect dog flew unto a rage.

"Before I'd do that to my dog, I'd quit hunting," he said, as he stalked off.

A month later, we held an informal trial, and the man was there to run his dog. He brought his 15 year old son along. While the man worked his dog, the son covered the dog with an air gun every second it was working. What's more, the dog knew it. He'd keep glancing back at the boy. Once, the boy's arms got tired, and he lowered the gun. The dog took off for the next county.

The Inventor

About this time, an inventive fellow in our group tried to figure a way to throw a spark, in order to make his dog obey at a distance. He used a spark coil from an ancient Ford Model T car. But this didn't work. So he decided to electrify a long training rope.

He wired the training rope, and got his wife to sew some canvas into a carrying pack for batteries and spark coil. The training rope was attached to a special collar which had points to touch the dog's neck skin.

This was a Rube Goldbergian type of apparatus, and rather formidable in appearance. The training fraternity was quite breathless to see it in operation. When the day came for the test, a crowd gathered, and a live pheasant was "planted" ahead of the dog.

The dog picked up the scent of the pheasant and moved in to it. But the pheasant elected to run instead of flushing into the air. The man blew his whistle and yelled "hup." As expected, the dog ignored both commands. So his owner turned on the juice.

The dog jumped 20 feet in surprise. But the gadget was somehow not properly grounded. The owner got the same shock, and jumped 40. The dog was so surprised, he came to heel, and quit hunting for the day. And that ended the experiment.

Now it's been said that true inventions are always made in the proper scientific climate which means at the right time and place in history. My friend was trying to invent something 30 years too soon.

Today, there is an electronic dog trainer available which works on the principle of the walkie-talkie. The receiver is fastened to the dog's collar. And the owner can shock him when he refuses to obey, even at distances of 200 yards.

Training By Example

Retrieving is either instinctive, or is an aptitude, in many breeds of dogs. Yet even in those breeds, there are many dogs which dislike to retrieve game. They can be taught to do so. But the handler must understand dogs, and in particular, his own, if he is to teach the lesson successfully.

In the early days of the Springer Spaniel, most of the owners were novices. They did not know how to teach their dogs to retrieve. Sometimes they spoiled the dogs, in so far as this branch of training was concerned. So it happened that at all the early trials, there would be dogs which refused to retrieve. Sometimes they'd bring the game part way to the handler, then drop it.

This would cause acute embarrassment to the handler. The latter would be begging the dog to "fetch," while like as not the dog would be wagging his tail and gazing off into space. Begging would change to ordering, and then to shouting. The dog would continue to wag its tail. It would be well aware of the fact that its owner could not punish it in front of the gallery.

One of these early trials was held in a snow storm, yet a fair sized gallery was present. A dog refused to pick up the dead bird, a pigeon. After begging it for a time, its owner got permission from the judge to show the dog how to do it. He got down on his hands and knees in the driving snow, picked up the bird in his own mouth, and then carried it in his mouth, while still on hands and knees.

This mightily impressed the gallery, but had no visible effect upon the dog, who seemed pleased to escape an unpleasant task, and flattered that his owner would do it for him.

Smelling Error

At about that time, a championship Pointer and Setter trial was held in Ohio. One of the great dogs of his time was competing. He had swept the trials before him, starting on the Canadian prairies and working south. A large crowd of sportsmen came out to see him run.

Such trials are conducted in "heats," which may be from 20 minutes to two or three hours in duration. Two dogs are paired in a heat. At big events, the course will be continuous. That is, a new heat will begin where the last one ended, with the new pair of dogs working on over a fresh course.

Few people care to follow the dogs over long distances. Some ride on horses. The majority gather in the area where one heat finishes and the next one starts. So a large crowd had gathered to see the great dog complete his heat. The heat ended at a road, which was higher than the adjacent land. Thus, the gallery had a perfect view.

The great dog came galloping through an immense field of knee high grasses and weeds. The afternoon sun glinted off his white sides. The dog moved swiftly and gracefully, testing the wind for bird scents, and going to birdy cover with rare intelligence.

The big white and liver colored Pointer worked up toward the end of the field, and consequently quite close to the gallery. Far behind were judge and handler on horseback. The dog came to a staunch and steady point, tail stiffened out and pointing skyward at the proper angle, his left front foot lifted stylishly. He was close enough so that you could see his big rib cage expand and contract with his breathing.

Handler and judge whipped up their horses and galloped up. The former leaped from his horse, handed the reins to the field marshall and then circled warily in front of his dog. He beat the tall grass and light brush with his whip to flush the game, so tightly held at point by the great champion.

And then there began a tremendous squawking and cackling. The champion of the world had made the unforgiveable error of pointing a chicken, peacefully setting on her clutch of eggs.

Tall Story

Pointers and Setters are often called bird dogs, since they perform best on quail, partridge, and grouse. In Ohio, quail are considered song birds. The somewhat cynical axiom of Ohio hunters is: Give him 20 yards in which to sing. If no song, then he's no song bird, and you can bag him. The trouble with that maxim is, if it takes you 20 yards to make up your mind, he'll be gone before you can shoot.

Because of Ohio's feeling that song birds shouldn't be quarry for a hunter and his dog, many Ohio field trials for Pointers and Setters are conducted on pheasants. Depending upon the kind of a trial it is, the pheasants may or may not be shot.

At one small Ohio trial, the writer served as a judge. This was a walking trial, one in which the judges had to walk all heats. The dog which I was following was a Pointer. He disappeared over a hill, and when he did not come back onto the course, the owner and I went up over the hill to find the dog.

We found him, to our immense astonishment, out on the limb of an apple tree, pointing a pheasant. Of course, we screamed for witnesses, and shouted for someone to bring a camera. But the pheasant moved, the dog tried to move, teetered on the limb a moment, and then fell out of the tree. The pheasant flew away. And no one, of course, believes us.

As we reconstructed it, the pheasant was a weak flyer which had just been released for the trial. The dog had flushed him, probably feeling safe in doing so since he was out of sight of owner and judge. He must have chased the bird until it lit in the apple tree. But the apple tree had at some time been pushed partly over, and then had continued to grow that way. The dog had been able to scrabble up the slanting trunk, and onto the limb. There pheasant and dog must have eyed each other speculatively, until we came along to break up the play. If only we'd had even one witness!

The Cat Trainer

The late Martin Hogan was an internationally known dog trainer who, in later years, specialized in spaniel and retriever training. He came to Ohio by train one fall to compete at the Ravenna spaniel trials. He brought only one dog, the great Field Champion Wake's Snow Drift. The time was late fall, the weekend after Thanksgiving.

After the trial, many of the contestants came to my home. Hogan was included, and of course, Snow Drift. Other owners had left their dogs in cars. But since Hogan had come out by train, he had neither car nor dog crate. So Snow Drift came along into the house.

Corners were littered with boots, outercoats, heavy socks, mittens, and hats and caps. There were drinks, and empty soda water bottles, flasks and fifths, littered the table. Hogan did not drink. He stood quietly talking, or listening, with Snow Drift sitting as quietly at his feet.

No one ever knew quite how, or why, it happened. But Snow Drift suddenly leaped straight up, and lit sitting up in that litter of bottles and glasses. Not a glass or a bottle was disturbed. Hogan was sweating with embarrassment. He couldn't lift Snow Drift from the table without knocking over glasses and bottles.

Of course, the incident was greeted with shouts of

laughter and good natured bantering. Hogan was somehow heartened into taking a greater part in the revelry, though without drinking. He saw our tom cat, Muff, sleeping quietly in a corner.

"Riddle," he said, "I'd like to prove to you that I am the world's best animal trainer. I can even train cats."

He pulled out his handkerchief.

"I'll bet you $1 I can make that tom cat of yours retrieve this handkerchief to hand on the very first command."

The bet was immediately covered. Hogan dropped the handkerchief on the floor and then spoke sternly to the cat.

"Fetch!"

Now Muff was one of the world's toughest tom cats. He had been named Little Miss Muffet by the children. But that was before he had grown sufficiently to demonstrate that his name would have to be shortened to Muff. No one ever knew Muff to obey any command except one.

My wife would pick him up. She claimed that he talked with his tail. So she would command him to talk, and Muff would shake his tail, in anger perhaps, but still in an odd fashion. Now, he slept on, ignoring Hogan's command to fetch.

Hogan picked him up by the tail and held him above the handkerchief. Muff began to claw air frantically. Whereupon, Hogan lowered him to the handkerchief. Muff's furiously clawing front legs, claws fully extended, caught the handkerchief. Hogan lifted him to chest height, took the handkerchief, and then set Muff down with a pat, and an apology.

Martin won his dollar. Some said he had been cruel to Muff, and others that he'd been clever. Muff's feelings had been hurt, and he was not to be put off with an apology, which he probably didn't understand anyway.

Muff stalked about among the coats and hats on the floor, tail switching angrily. Probably, if there had not been so much noise in the house we could have heard the growls he used to make when he was angry.

He found what he wanted—Hogan's hat, resplendent with field trial badges pinned to the band. He backed up to it and sprayed it with the horrible, yellow, impossible to get out urine, so typical of tom cats.

Hogan laughed.

"He's the winner," he said. "It'll cost me more than a dollar to get that hat cleaned and odorless enough to wear again."

8

Dog Tales

THE TWINS

The best dog sale I ever made? That's easy!

This guy's nickname is Insane, which he often is, though he gets the moniker on account of the dog. The dog's nickname is Sane, which maybe he isn't. But he gets it on account of the man. And they both get these nicknames at an insane asylum, where everyone calls them The Twins, Sane and Insane.

It came about thusly.

I have an English Springer Spaniel named Sweet Marie. When she comes in season, I make up my mind to breed her to a champion named White Cloud. He is owned in a big kennel about 100 miles away. So I drive over there with Sweet Marie.

The kennel owner greets me with happiness, because we are friends. And besides, he will get $35 for the mating. He brings out a bottle which, he assures me, has just been smuggled in from Canada. We drink quite a bit and discuss many things. We finally get around to discuss this mating.

"Why don't you breed your bitch to Huntsman?" he asks. "I think he is a better dog than White Cloud. And the stud fee is the same."

But I think that Sweet Marie does not have heavy enough leg bone. And she has certain hunting faults which should not be named. I think White Cloud will correct these.

"He will too," the man agrees. "But sometimes he sires pups that are a bit on the large size. Mind now, rough and tough hunting dogs. But also hard headed."

I am of the opinion I can train a hard headed dog. And once he is trained, he will stay trained. And he will not quit in briars or freezing sleet. Things like that. So I am all the more convinced that White Cloud is the perfect mate for Sweet Marie.

I demand to see him, and this makes my friend embarrassed. Here he has this fine, modern, heated kennel with runs and all conveniences. And here are 50 dogs, champions, brood bitches, and puppies. But no White Cloud. So then he was to admit that he is short of space, and he is keeping White Cloud in a pen with some goats.

85

This is cause for astonishment in me.

"Aren't you afraid that billy goat will butt him to death?"

"No," he says. "That White Cloud isn't afraid of goats—or dogs." He adds the dogs as a sort of after thought. "That dog can take care of himself anywhere, and with any thing."

I do not get the significance of this at the time, because I am impressed by this dog, White Cloud. So is Sweet Marie. The mating is made immediately, and with no trouble, which is most unusual for her.

One day in late March, we get a snow storm. And the coal man comes with a load of coal. I have fixed up a Whelping bed for Sweet Marie right next to the coal bin. And it is at this moment of inconvenience that she whelps her puppies. I am much afraid that the noise will give those pups a mental block, or that Sweet Marie will get excited and kill her puppies.

However, nothing much happens. I give the coal man a couple of snorts of my own Canadian bootleg, and he holds off until the second pup is born, which is all Sweet Marie has. One puppy is orange and white, and this is frowned upon in the best Springer Spaniel circles. The other is a well marked liver and white. Both are males.

By the time these puppies are five weeks old, they are trying to kill each other. And by the time they are eight, it is obvious that they will do so when they get a bit larger and stronger. It is also obvious that they are going to grow up to be monsters in size. My wife keeps telling me to do something before they do. I am aware that for once she is not just being prejudiced against dogs, and is probably right.

To admit that she is right is not proper, of course, or even wise. However, I trade the orange and white pup for the down payment on an electric stove. This makes my wife overjoyed. But it is also a good deal in itself, and maybe the next best sale I ever made.

The stove salesman is a hunting companion of mine. Or, a drinking companion, as my wife puts it. He is a fine aviator who has been grounded for an error in judgment. He has overestimated his alcoholic capacity, and has buzzed the Kentucky Derby. This has made a lot of people unhappy. The stove selling business is very poor at this time, because

Roosevelt has not had time to bring back liquor and good times. So my friend is most happy to get a hunting dog, and to sell a stove as well.

The other pup I keep, figuring I will make him into a field trial dog, or at the very least, into a hunting dog. I name him Sain. A Mongolian word, I am told, meaning both Hello and Goodbye. This Sain seems to have a born capacity to hunt, and he hits water like a wild goose.

But then, there is not so much game that summer, especially pheasants. And I wish to give Sain as much work as possible on pheasants while he is still very young. So when he is four months old, I send him to a trainer who lives on a pheasant preserve, and will give Sain that work. Later, I will put the fine points into his style.

At the end of the first month, I get a letter from this trainer, to wit:

'Come' and get your dog. He half kills every dog in the kennel, and he bites out a chunk of tongue of an Irish Water Spaniel twice his size. The owner of this Irish Water Spaniel loves this dog like a baby, and they sleep together. And he says he is going to sue us both.

"I think I can calm him down with a fifth of Scotch. But somebody is going to have to pay the veterinary bill and for the Scotch. And I think it is going to be you.

"Your dog," he adds, "is not mean or vicious. He just likes to taste other dogs. And in proof of same, he wags his tail all the time he is fighting."

So I am reading this letter in the post office when long comes this loco friend. He is in a most happy mood, swinging his arms and talking in a shout, and grinning so he could swallow a pond. He wishes to buy a trained Springer Spaniel for a hunting dog, and he says I am his man to find one for him.

I explain to him that fully trained dogs are impossible to buy. But I add that I think I have just the dog for him. He is a good hunting dog, I tell him, though at this point I am not sure if he is a good one, or only could be.

I am careful to be completely honest with him though. I tell him that this is a fine young dog which, in spite of his youth, likes to fight upon occasion. But I will sacrifice him for a small veterinary bill, the cost of a month's training, and one fifth of Scotch. Total: $50.50.

This pleases the man very greatly. He grins wider than ever, swings his arms, and talks in his loudest shouting voice.

"So he likes to mix things up, does he? Well, confidentially," he roars, so the whole town can hear him, "I like to abuse people myself. I have crazy spells because I have bugs in my blood. And when the bugs get going, so do I. It might just be that this dog and I will get along fine together."

I agree that I will give him a demonstration of this dog the coming weekend, when I have brought him back from the training kennel. But I am worried. I am sure this dog can hunt but I do not know how much work this trainer has given him.

"Do not worry about that," the trainer says, pocketing my check for $50.50. "This dog can hunt like he can fight. Which is to say he is going to steal all the hunting area from any other dog along. And he is going to make every other dog's retrieve, or die trying. And that dog ain't going to die very sudden."

So comes Saturday, and the man shows up to see the demonstration. But before I can do so, my loco friend looks over the dog with great satisfaction.

"What's his name?, " he asks.

"Sain," I reply.

The man doubles right up with laughter, slapping his sides and shouting, and pounding me on the back until I am coughing for breath.

"He's sane and I'm insane," he shouts.

Right then, he refuses to see the dog work out. He doesn't care if the dog can or cannot hunt. With this name, the dog just has to be his. He puts the dog in the car, and off they go, with Sain barking his fool head off.

These two are inseparable instantly. And they hunt together in season and out. The toughest game warden in the state is in our county. And it seems as though he is always on our trail. He figures that, if you are training dogs, you are just naturally going to knock off a quail or pheasant occasionally. Now the fellows are all law abiding citizens. But it is true that a dog cannot hunt day after day without a reward for effort. The game warden is most unreasonable not to see this.

However, he just ignores Sain and his master. There isn't a covey of quail in the county which hasn't lost a member or two. The pheasants just seem to migrate to some other county. But, on the other hand, the man's periods of insanity are farther apart, and they do not last so long.

But when he does go loco, they can't get him to the mental hospital without the dog. The hospital superintendent says he is not about to make his institution a haven for dogs and cats. He howls loud and long. But these are depression years, and private mental institutions charge high rates.

Besides, the patients quickly name them Sane and Insane. This vastly amuses the man, and maybe even the dog. For he seems to love the other patients almost as insanely as he does his master. When the long term and permanent patients see them coming, they set up an excited roar for Sane and Insane. The hospital superintendent admits that patient morale goes up 20 per cent right there. So he makes an exception and allows Sain to come as a free, if star boarder.

The last time Insane is there, the hospital sends word he is ready to come home. But his wife cannot go after him. It is only 40 miles to the hospital. So she sends a taxi, and I go along to keep the driver company.

Sane and Insane are ready to leave, and all the inmates come out to see them off. Insane is roaring and beaming, and Sane is in his lap, paws on his shoulders, and looking out the back window. He is barking excitedly at all the friends he is leaving behind. The hospital morale drops 20 points.

A couple of weeks later, I meet this taxi driver, and he is fuming.

I am becoming nothing but a chauffeur for a dog," he laments. "I get a call to go to Insane's house, and when I get there, he is taking a bath, and shouting and singing so you can hear him two blocks away with the windows closed, which they are not.

"And the maid opens the door and hands that Sane out on a leash, and gives me a note.

"Please take my baby doll out to the dog hospital and have them give him a bath. Then call back for him."

"Baby doll, Hell," he mutters. "Only yesterday, I seen that German Shepherd Dog of Joe Black's going down the street, and he is beating Man O' War's record for six furlongs. Only he ain't gonna win by no nose. Because this Sane is after him. And he has his tail plastered under him so far, it is out in front of his nose."

Well, after he thinks this over awhile, he feels better. There was a $5 bill pinned to that note. The taxi trip is only $1.50 both ways, and the bath is $2. So he clears an extra $1.50. Besides, Joe Black has been bragging what a great fighter his dog is. So it is worth something to chauffeur around a dog which has shut up Joe Black and whipped his dog all at one time.

Sane is about eight years old when it ends. He is huge heavily muscled. And there isn't a dog that will come within six blocks of Insane's house. When they aren't hunting, they are taking walks together. And Sane even sleeps with Insane, taking up the middle of the bed.

It ends one summer afternoon. There is a picnic table in the big back yard, and behind that, an old carriage barn with the stalls and mangers, and even some of the harness gathering dust on hooks in the walls of the carriage room.

Sane and Insane are sitting on the picnic table. The table is getting some shade from a big oak tree. Sane and Insane aren't doing anything. Just sitting there and looking. But not looking at anything in particular. Just sort of drinking the summer day. And the man has his arm around the dog.

It is time for Insane to go. He just falls forward off the table, bounces off the bench, and lies there on the ground, dead. His wife sees it happen and rushes out from the house. But Sain is standing over the body, and will not let her near.

People gather, and Sain stands guard, growling savagely at those who approach. But finally a man who has hunted many times with the two of them comes up. He chases the others away, and then talks quietly to Sain. And finally, he is able to put a leash on him and lead him away.

He does not know what to do with him. So he takes him into the old barn. There is a tie chain and snap still fastened to one manger. Sain is wearing a choke collar, and so he just snaps the chain to the collar, and leaves the dog there.

Then they call me and ask if I will come for Sain and care for him until it is decided what to do with him. I go immediately. But Sain is dead. He has gone berserk in his grief and has got tangled in the chain. He has choked to death.

All the boys who had known and hunted with them gather at the pool hall that night. They speak of them in awe, and particularly of Sain, and his strange death. Some say they should be buried together. But the minister, who likes a gun and dog, and has hunted with them himself, says it would cause a scandal.

So we bury Sain in the pasture beside Sweet Marie. And the kids make a small cross. They get a crayon and scrawl his name on it. Only they spell it as they had known him—SANE.

COMEDY OR TRAGEDY

There is no clearly distinguishable line dividing comedy and tragedy, any more than there are lines dividing the colors of the spectrum. Many of the incidents in this book will be said to be funny. For myself, I cannot tell which are funny and which are tragic. Perhaps the two are separated by a middle zone of pathos, or bathos, and even of sweetness.

A doctor in our town was once visited by a man and woman from Canada. The doctor had known both man and wife during his youth. He liked the man, but disliked the woman. The couple had brought along a Boston Terrier, then about a year old. It was the man's delight. Probably because of his affection for the dog, the woman detested it.

The man appeared to love his wife. But she was a greedy, stingy, and nasty tempered woman who was waiting only for her husband to die. He obliged her while visiting in our town. She showed little signs of grief. She made the necessary arrangements for shipping her husband's body home, and then decreed that the dog should die.

The dog had been her husband's, not hers, she said. And she had no affection for it. She frankly said that she wanted nothing that had been her husband's property, except for his estate. And she added that she had no intention of spending a penny more on a worthless, dirty, dog.

On the other hand, she imagined that it might cost as much as $15 to have the dog put to death and its body buried. The doctor imagined that it would. Would he do it himself so that she could save that much money? He would not. If she gave him the $15, would he have the job done for her? He would. Whereupon, she gave him the money and departed for Canada.

But the doctor did not have the dog killed. He had her spayed instead. And then he bought a fine bed and dog harness for her. He kept her until she died of old age 13 years later.

The dog would sleep in its bed while the doctor was at home. But when he was out, she would sit on a small table at the front window and watch for him. Going down the street at night, you could always tell when the doctor was out on a call. And it gave you a happy feeling to see the dog waiting there, not sleeping, not lying down, just sitting there quietly and watching.

It would comfort the doctor, too, to see the dog sitting there. When he had taken off his coat, he would pick her up. She would nuzzle him happily, and then settle in his lap as he stroked her. The doctor's shoulders would straighten a little, and he would feel the tenseness in his body evaporating.

At a tenderly given command, the dog would go quietly off to her bed. And as the doctor crawled into his own bed, he'd think happily of the revenge he'd received in the name of his dead friend.

Everyone knows of some old lady who has kept a cat. And the cat has kittens. Soon the old person will have a mess of cats. Friends will shake their heads sadly, and avoid the house because of the odor.

I once investigated the case of a boarder with an ulcer. He complained to his doctor that his landlady fed him contaminated food. The doctor reported the matter to the sanitary police. The man with the ulcer had also complained that his landlady had 72 cats, and this proved to be no exaggeration.

Some years before, when the woman had had only a dozen cats, neighbors had complained to the sanitary police. The police had ordered the woman to dispose of all but two of the cats. But she had been unable to decide which cats to keep and which to put to sleep.

It was a cruel choice to have to make, so she avoided making it. Instead, at great expense, she had an elevator made. It ran from the basement to the third floor attic. It was cleverly concealed with a facing which made it look like a no longer used brick chimney.

Cats are not easy to train. So it can be imagined how difficult it was to teach them to use the elevator. She taught them to scat for the elevator each time she struck a chime They would then be transported to the attic.

The police returned to see if she had obeyed orders. They found no cats. They made a third visit, upon a second complaint. No cat were found. But then, the cat population exploded to 72. And, although the woman kept windows and doors closed, summer and winter, the odor seeped out and was wafted into nearby homes.

On the fourth visit, the sanitary police had knowledge of the elevator. So they found the surprised cats in the attic. This time the woman did not have to make a choice. Humane officers seized all the cats.

This was, of course, tragic for the cats. But the woman recovered surprisingly well. After a suitable period of wailing, she cleaned herself up; had the house deodorized by industrial engineers; and then got married. And her new husband—20 years her junior—was the boarder with the ulcer. He got her a dog for a wedding present.

Another lady of my acquaintance once kept a field trial crowd spellbound while she told us of her Weimaraners. Each night, it was the job of the butler to give five of the dogs a witch hazel and oil rubdown, not to mention a once a week bath.

After the rubdown, the five dogs were brought to the bedroom. One slept on the pillow beside her; one in the middle of the bed; and a third at the foot. Two others occupied chairs placed beside the bed.

The lady related this with pride. She had avoided dog fights by teaching each dog its special place. It had torn her heart strings, she said, to have to decide which dog should have the honor of sharing the pillow beside her. For that's where each dog wanted to be.

The woman's husband was present when she related this. All of us wondered where he slept. But he did not volunteer the information, nor did his wife.

The following story is reprinted here as it appeared in the Cleveland Press for Aug. 10, 1950. It is correct, but is lacking in one detail which will be given later.

"This story involves three families, 17 dogs, and five chickens at a small, two-story tenement dwelling at 2567 E. 73rd St.

"Mrs. Jennie Rose, 53, 17 years a widow, owns the building and lives downstairs. She has 15 dogs. One of the upstairs tenants, Joe Glasco, has two dogs and the chickens. The third tenant has none.

"Mrs. Rose has the yard fenced, but neighbors have complained about the barking and the stench. An earlier complaint last February, charged the dogs served as a flea hatchery for the entire neighborhood.

"Sanitary Inspector Henry Cavanagh investigated the second complaint. He said Mrs. Rose had given her bed to the dogs, and was sleeping in a chair. He also said one of the dogs tried to bite him.

"The Sanitation Department ordered Mrs. Rose to get rid of the dogs, and the odor, within 10 days. Mrs. Glasco was ordered to get rid of her chickens.

"Mrs. Rose said she would get rid of all but four of her dogs.

"Said Mrs. Glasco: 'If she's allowed to keep some of her dogs, I'm going to keep my chickens.' Mrs. Rose was not ordered to dispose of her own dogs.

"Dog Wardens Adolph Simon and Elmer Bruck said they found all the dogs well fed. They said Mrs. Rose had spent $52 for dog licenses.

" 'They charged me for one too many,' Mrs. Rose complained.

" 'Well, you're lucky we didn't arrest you,' Simon said. 'You got a male license for a female dog and gypped us out of $2.'

"'Yes,' said Mrs. Rose, 'I just forgot. When you have so many . . . ' Her voice trailed off.

"Friends said they would find homes in the country for all the dogs Mrs. Rose was willing to give up."

What should be added to this story is that these same friends had smuggled 10 pups out of the house before the sanitary police and dog wardens arrived.

The following Associated Press dispatch concerned a dog fancier and author who was well known to the dog writers and breeders of the time.

"Riverside, Cal., Mar. 16, 1950—Mrs. Helene Arlington, writer of dog stories, says she will ask the courts to annul her marriage to her landscape gardner, on the grounds the union was not consummated, because she took a chastity vow when she was a young girl.

"The 38 year-old author of "DEAR DOG LADY" and her husband, Masefield Thomas Arlington, 53, embraced Buddhism after their marriage in 1949. But she says: 'The real stumbling block to our marriage is that he really isn't a Buddhist, and I couldn't live with a Christian.'

"Arlington changed his name from Charles Thomas Olson before the marriage, because she did not want to lose her identity as writer of such books as PAWPRINTS ON MY HEART and others.

"Mrs. Arlington keeps 21 Dalmatian dogs on her Riverside County ranch, which has no telephone, no electricity, no transportation, and no visitors."

Note: The two were later re-married.

Since, at the beginning of this book I admitted to the charge of being the craziest of the dog people, I should here tell this tragi-comic incident on myself.

Our Springer Spaniel, Annie, was a slut, or a jade, or a wench. Whichever of the terms you'd care to use, she was it. Let any male sniff around her when she was not in heat, and she'd tear him apart. But, the very day she'd come in heat, she'd run away and stay until mated.

Normally, Annie would stay in her kennel run without fuss, and without trying to get out. Still, she was an escape artist of unusual cunning and resourcefulness. And a special pen was needed for her when she came in heat.

On one occasion, however, the problem was not one of keeping Annie in, but of keeping another dog out. The nearest neighbor is three quarters of a mile away, and has no dog. Our own male dogs were safely shut in their own kennel runs, 50 yards away. So there should have been no problem.

But one morning, we awoke to find that a German Shepherd had climbed the fence, crossed the angled-in top wire which kept Annie from climbing out, and then had dropped into the pen. In 63 days, Annie whelped 10 pups.

The world is full of unwanted mongrel puppies, and these usually end in the execution chamber of an animal shelter after a shorter or longer life of misery. So in this case, we were prepared. Annie whelped the puppies at a veterinary hospital. As each was born, the veterinarian put it to sleep. After the last one, Annie was given a hormone shot to prevent milk from forming. And in a few days, she was at home again, as happy as ever.

But my wife was cross about this. No more puppies, she said. And she repeated this again and again the next time Annie came in heat. And yet I had an excellent male, named Rye, who would make a suitable mate for Annie. So on a fine afternoon, while my wife was on a shopping trip, I just happened to let Rye into the segregation pen with Annie. Of course, I said nothing of this to my wife.

I figured that she would just happen to notice some day that that Annie was "that way" again. And by the time I would get home from the office, half the shock would be over. Then one day, while I was at the office, Cal Barry called to borrow Annie for his dog act at the winter sportsmen's show. My wife knew that I would approve this. So Cal took Annie along, and I had no chance to tell him that she was probably pregnant. I did not worry about this. Cal would find out soon enough.

But Cal took the act on the road before I had a chance to warn him. And later, I had to go to the hospital for an operation. I was sicker, and sick longer, than I had anticipated. On the day of my release, my wife drove to Cleveland to bring me home.

"I forgot to tell you," she said, as we drove along, "Annie had 11 puppies a couple of days ago."

"Is that so," I exclaimed, hoping I showed proper surprise. "Are they over at Cal's kennels?"

"No," she said. "I knew they were mongrels. So I had Cal take her to the veterinary hospital. He destroyed the pups as fast as they were born. The way you did with the last litter."

Telephone Call: "I am allergic to dogs. But I just had to have a dog, so I bought a Miniature Schnauzer puppy. My allergist is furious. What can I do?"

"Well, there are a number of products which you can spray on the dog. They will keep down dog dander for a week."

"But I'm not allergic to dog dander. I'm allergic to coliform bacteria in the dog's stools."

I have never heard this before, and I am stunned with surprise. Finally, I tell her she should always take her puppy outside to the same spot and then stay up wind.

This problem was so startling that I consulted an allergist who raises Newfoundland dogs. His father, an allergist before him, had been an animal hater. So he always told *his* patients to get rid of any animals—whether dogs, cats, canaries, or even goldfish—regardless of whether they were allergic or not to any animals.

So I told him this story. And wishing to show my own knowledge of allergies, I remarked: "The allergist who tracked this one down was a real detective."

Silence for a minute. Then: "He was a damn liar. If she is allergic to coliform bacteria in the dog's stool, she's allergic to those in her own and they'll kill her."

9

The Great International

Dog Deal

YES SIR, I HAVE YOUR LETTER RIGHT HERE.

Potchefstroom, Transvaal
Union of South Africa
Jan. 2, 1952

Dear Mr. Riddle:

You do not know me, and I don't know you. And perhaps you will think this an imposition. But I have met a man down here who says he used to read your dog column in the Cleveland Press when he was living in Akron.

He says he does not know you, but he believes you to be a man of honour, and he says you know more about dogs than anyone else. He says if I want to buy an American dog, I should not hesitate to write to you, as you are known to help all people with dog problems.

Now I want to buy a Boxer female. I have been studying up on American Boxers. Most of your big breeders want more money that I can afford to pay, and also, I am afraid they will send me a poor dog. They could figure that a dog can't be returned from South Africa, so that this would be a chance to unload a cull.

I want to get a bitch of Brandy bloodlines, bred to Ch. Bang Away of Sirrah Crest. She must be Canadian owned. The reason she must be Canadian owned is that I have a permit to export up to $500 to Canada. But I cannot get a permit to export the money to the United States.

Also, there is a six months quarantine period for American dogs here. But I can get a veterinary permit to bring in a dog from Canada without making the dog go through the quarantine period. This is because there is no rabies in Canada.

I want a very dark red or brindle, and I want her to have some white on her. The reason is, most of the boxers here are a very washed out fawn, and they have no white on them, or very little.

Anxiously awaiting your reply, I am

Your Humble Servant,
Wilfrid MacKenzie

Cleveland Ohio
Jan. 12, 1952

Dear Mr. MacKenzie:

I have your letter of Jan. 2, and I am happy to say that I will do what I can.

As you say, Boxers are riding the crest here now, and it is difficult to buy one which can win at shows, and which will be bred to our best champion, at any price near $500.

Your request presents other difficulties, too. Bang Away is in Southern California, where he is at stud at a very high price, with no return in case of failure. It will be difficult to discover whether there is a good bitch of Brandy bloodlines in Canada, or at any rate, in eastern Canada, where I might have a chance to see her.

Obviously, if we were to locate a good Brandy daughter, say in Nova Scotia, the cost of shipping her to California, plus the stud fee, would eat up most of the $500.

However, I am going over to Canada to judge a show in the near future, and I will make some discreet inquiries. This is most difficult for me, because American dog judges are not allowed to engage in the buying and selling of dogs for profit. I will be doing this as a labor of love, but I do not want any misunderstanding to arise. I'll report to you, as soon as I have anything worth reporting.

Sincerely,
Maxwell Riddle

Canine World Magazine
Detroit 16, Mich.

Mar. 13, 1952

Dear Mr. Riddle:

I am enclosing a letter from Mr. Wilfrid MacKenzie of Potchefstroom, Transvaal, South Africa, which is self explanatory. For business reasons, I do not handle things like this. But I am certain you can—and will. Please report to me on this matter.

Very truly,
Harold Worstel, Editor

Potchefstroom, Transvaal
Union of South Africa
Mar. 1, 1952

The Editor
Canine World Magazine
Detroit 16, Mich.

Dear Mr. Worstel:

I wish to buy a bred Boxer bitch on your side of the Atlantic. I have written to another person, but I have heard nothing for a long time. So I am asking your help.

I want a deep red or brindle bitch, good enough to win over here. She must be of Brandy bloodline, bred to Ch. Bang Away of Sirrah Crest. And she must be Canadian owned because of certain import restrictions here.

Can you help me? Or can you refer me to someone who can, and who will see that I get honest treatment?

Your Humble Servant,
Wilfrid MacKenzie

Canine World Magazine
Detroit 16, Mich.
Mar. 13, 1952

Dear Mr. MacKenzie:

Unfortunately, for business reasons, I do not engage in these transactions. However, I am referring you to Mr. Maxwell Riddle, Cleveland Press, Cleveland, O. He likes to help people, and I am sure that he will take care of you. I am asking him to report to me on progress, so that he will not let the matter slide.

Very Truly Yours,
Harold Worstel, Editor

Cleveland, Ohio
Mar. 18, 1952

Dear Mr. MacKenzie:

I have your letter to Mr. Worstel, and his reply, and wish to state that I am working on the problem. However, you have given me a large order. And even assuming I can find the proper bitch, we will have to wait until she comes in season. Since dogs don't do that at human whim, it might even take five months or more of waiting after we have located her.

In the meantime, I have made some inquiries in Canada. I have not found any bitches of Brandy bloodlines yet. But I have seen some Bang Away puppies. One problem I vision is this. Suppose we mate a bitch to Bang Away, and then send her to you, only to find that the mating didn't take? I can't see myself sending you a bred bitch, and then having her turn up barren after you get her.

Meanwhile, if you could just arrange to send the money to the United States, perhaps the quarantine problem could be solved.

For instance, have you checked the quarantine regulations? I assume the bitch would be quarantined at Durban. Now American dogs going to Hawaii are quarantined there for four months. But if the dog is a bitch in whelp, special rules apply. The bitch stays four months, but the pups can be taken out as soon as weaned.

Well, have patience, I'm working on this.

Sincerely,
Maxwell Riddle

Potchefstroom, Transvaal
Union of South Africa
Mar. 30, 1952

Dear Mr. Riddle:

Thank you for your letter. I wrote to Harold Worstel because I thought you had given me up when I didn't hear from you.

No, I can't arrange the quarantine thing as you suggest. Nor can I export the money to the United States. Another reason I worry is that the veterinary permit I got will expire Sept. 1. So I have to have the dog in my possession before then.

I feel sure that with your connections, you can work all this out though.

Your Humble Servant,
Wilfrid MacKenzie

Dear Mr. MacKenzie:

I have been working on your problem, but I don't see any hope under the conditions you lay down for me.

But I have thought of an alternate plan. Let me try to find the sort of bitch you want in the United States. I have friends in Canada, and I would ask them to help me out.

I would send the bitch over to Canada, and have her registration transferred to the Canadian Kennel Club, with ownership to a Canadian friend of mine. Then my friend would export the dog to you. The dog would have a Canadian owner, and registration transfer would come from the Canadian National Livestock Records, direct to you.

You could send the money to my friend, and my friend in turn, could send the money to the American owner. In that way, you would have your dog, and everyone would be happy.

Sincerely,
Maxwell Riddle

Potchefstroom, Transvaal
Union of South Africa
May 20, 1952

Dear Mr. Riddle:

Your idea sounds fine to me, and I suggest you go ahead along those lines. But please remember that I want a very good bitch, and one that can win the shows down here. But I don't think our Boxers are the equal of yours. So it needn't be the best bitch in the United States.

The reason I want one from your side is that we have Boxers here from England, Switzerland, and Germany. And I don't believe they are as good as yours in the United States.

I am anxiously awaiting the fruition of your new plans, and I am much encouraged in my project.

Your Humble Servant,
Wilfrid MacKenzie

Telephone Call: June 5, 1952

Operator: Here's your party in Pittsburgh. Go ahead.

Riddle: Hello. Mr. Mulvey?

Mulvey: Yes, this is Mulvey. Who are you?

Riddle: This is Maxwell Riddle at the Cleveland Press. I hear you want to sell that red bitch of yours.

Mulvey: I hadn't thought about it. But I might consider selling her. That is, to the right party. Who wants to buy her?

Riddle: I have an inquiry from a breeder in South Africa. Tell me. How is she bred?

Mulvey: She's beautifully bred. She's by Brandy, out of a daughter of Monarch's Ego.

Riddle: Sounds good. When is she coming in season?

Mulvey: She's in season now. I bred her today to Champion Warbird of Azuza, the California dog. He's here in my kennel for the moment. And I plan to breed her to him again tomorrow.

Riddle: That's great. The South African wants her bred in this country anyway. How much do you want for her?

Mulvey: Well, I don't know that I want to sell her to a

104

	South African. I don't want her living in any old steaming tropical jungle. It doesn't sound so good to me.
Riddle:	But this man lives in Potchefstroom in the Transvaal. It's nearly 2000 feet above sea level, and it's said to have the most even climate in the world. Besides, there aren't any jungles or sleeping sickness flies, and that sort of thing that far south.
Mulvey:	Well, but it would take months to get her there. And she might get dropped off in some tropical seaport, and have her puppies there.
Riddle:	No, I checked the airlines. Pan American has a flight straight through from New York. It only takes three days. Maybe even less.
Mulvey:	Well, okay. I might sell her for $500.
Riddle:	Wonderful! But the man can only spend $500. Would you make it $475? Then we could get a shipping crate and stay fairly close to the $500 limit which he can get out of the country.
Mulvey:	Well, okay, I'll do it. It ought to be worth something for me to have a dog of my breeding down there.
Riddle:	Wonderful! Now this will involve some doing, because this man can't export his money to the United States. But he has a permit to export that much to Canada. So we'll have to transfer the dog to Canadian ownership, and then have the Canadian ship her. But I'll write you all the details. Good bye.

CABLEGRAM
June 5, 1952

Wilfrid MacKenzie
Potchefstroom, Transvaal
Union of South Africa

Can get you Brandy daughter, bred to Champion Warbird of Azuza. Stop. Letter following.

Maxwell Riddle

Cleveland Press
Cleveland, Ohio
June 5, 1952

Dear Mr. MacKenzie:

As per my cable of this date, I have made arrangements today, pending your approval, to purchase a very good bitch, Hofbrau's Juniper Queen. She is a daughter of Brandy, and is out of a bitch by Champion Monarch's Ego of Garakonti. Moreover, she has a double cross to German Champion Arnulf von Thorheim, which is the most desired blood in America. Also, she has won half the required championship points, including both the needed major victories.

She's bred to the very good Champion Warbird of Azuza, a California dog who is from the famed Canyonaire Kennels breeding. The price is $475. This will leave some money for purchase of a crate. But shipment to Canada, and similar expense might come to $60 additional.

Please advise by cable, since time will be short to do everything we must.

Sincerely,
Maxwell Riddle

CABLEGRAM

Potschefstroom Transvaal June 11, 1952.
Sounds good.   Stop.   Go ahead.   MacKenzie.

Phone Call: June 12, 1952

Operator: I have Mr. Turnbull of the Canadian Kennel Club for you. Go ahead.

Riddle: Is that you Frank? How are you?

Turnbull: Fine. Glad to hear from you. But it must be important for you to telephone.

Riddle: It is. I have a man in South Africa who wants to buy a bred Boxer bitch. I have located the bitch for him. But he can't export the money to the United States. Only to Canada. And besides, there is a quarantine on American dogs over there. But none on Canadian dogs.

Turnbull: But where do I fit into that picture?

Riddle: I want to transfer the dog to a reliable Canadian owner who will, in turn, transfer her to the South African. And who will also ship her for me.

Turnbull: Well, it sounds a little complicated to me. But, if all I have to do is to recommend someone, I suggest Mrs. Winifred Burns. She lives near the border at Buffalo, and is used to taking dogs back and forth across the border at Buffalo.

Riddle: Oh sure, I know Mrs. Burns very well. I'll write to her today. But time will be short. Will it be possible to get the papers through in a few days?

Turnbull: That is up to the Canadian National Livestock Records. But Mrs. Burns can probably handle it for you.

Riddle: Thanks for the suggestions. I'll go to work on them right away.

Welland, Ontario
June 15, 1952

Dear Max:

Yours with the long story at hand. I'll be glad to help. You will have to ship the dog to our mutual friend at Buffalo, Bob Harrison. I will then drive over to Buffalo and pick her up. Bob and I have been through customs so many times, we know most of the angles to escaping red tape at the border.

Two copies of her pedigree must be included. Also, a health certificate, and a certificate showing rabies vaccination. I am enclosing registration application for the Canadian National Livestock Records, and also nose print forms. Two prints are required, and they must be clear.

I know Harry Hubertson at the Canadian National Livestock Records personally. I will call him up, explain that the bitch has been bred, and ask a quick transfer of papers. He doesn't process the papers himself, except as in such a case as this. So he won't know about the quick transfer to someone else's ownership.

107

When shipping arrangements are made, I can drive the dog to Malton Airport at Toronto, which is only 100 miles from here. I expect Mr. MacKenzie will have to have his bank send a draft to mine, which is the Welland Branch of the Imperial Bank of Canada.

Let me know exactly what you want me to do, and I'll try my best to get the little girl safely on her way.

Sincerely,
Winnie

Pittsburgh, Pa.
June 18, 1952

Dear Riddle:

Just how the Hell do I get a dog nose printed, and where? And another thing. Queenie is a young bitch, and she's never been mated before. How will I know she's pregnant? I'm not going to send her all the way to South Africa and then not have her come forth with anything. I have my own reputation to protect.

I await your instructions on this. But personally, I think you are either a madman or a genius, if you think you can get away with this.

Yours truly,
Frank Mulvey

Cleveland, Ohio
June 19, 1952

Dear Mr. Mulvey:

The only thing you can do is to take her to a police station. Maybe the finger print expert will make the prints for you. But for goodness' sake, go to a suburban station. We don't want any newspapermen and photographers snooping around. The story and her picture might get to South Africa.

As for the pregnancy. Some veterinarians know how to palpate the abdomen of bitches to tell if they are carrying puppies. I suggest you take Queenie to one you trust, and ask him to try it.

Hard words, that madman stuff.

Sincerely,
Maxwell Riddle

TELEGRAM
June 21, 1952

Maxwell Riddle
Cleveland Press
Cleveland, Ohio

No vet here can palpate her at this stage. Any suggestions, genius?

Mulvey

TELEGRAM
June 21, 1952

Frank Mulvey
Trucheon Kennels
Pittsburgh, Pa.

Yes. They use a rabbit pregnancy test on human beings. Why not on dogs?

Riddle

Pittsburgh, Pa.
June 25, 1952

Dear Riddle:

First of all, I took Queenie to the Sewickley police station, where I know the chief personally. He performed the nose print operation, and we got good impressions. Quite a crowd gathered. But I didn't tell them why we wanted the prints.

But I have bad news for you. The vet here states flatly that Queenie is not pregnant. He got a rabbit and performed the pregnancy test. It was negative. But then he discovered that he had used a buck rabbit, and the test won't work, negative.

So that means the deal is off. Too bad! You had a complicated dream going there.

Sincerely,
Frank Mulvey

Telephone Call

Riddle: Western Reserve University? I'd like to speak to Dr. Barney, please.

Dr. Barney: Hello. Yes?

Riddle: Dr. Barney, I'd like to know whether or not the rabbit pregnancy test will work on dogs?

Dr. Barney: Who the hell are you, wanting to know the answer to a silly question like that?

Riddle: This is Maxwell Riddle of the Cleveland Press. I admit the question sounds silly. But I have to learn whether or not this bitch is pregnant before shipping her to South Africa.

Dr. Barney: Oh, I see. Well, I'm sorry if I spouted off. But, of course the pregnancy test won't work on dogs. The hormone balances are different. You get negative tests every time. And nobody's ever been interested enough to work out the tests for dogs.

Riddle: Thank you, Dr. Barney. You've been a big help.

110

TELEGRAM
June 26, 1952

Frank Mulvey
Truncheon Kennels
Pittsburgh, Pa,
Western Reserve University scientists
say rabbit pregnancy test won't work on dogs
because of difference in hormone balances.
Results always negative. Deal still on.
We'll await natural developments.
Riddle

25 June, 1952
Potschefstroom, South Africa

Dear Mr. Riddle:

I have made arrangements with Pan American Airways to receive the dog in New York for shipment to Palmeifontein Airdrome, Johannesburg. Pan American has notified its New York office to expect the dog about July 20. But you will have to notify the New York office as to the exact date. You must have a reservation to avoid shipping delay.

Also, I have placed more than adequate fees with Transvaal Cartage Co. Ltd., in Johannesburg. And it has notified Pan American that it will guarantee payment of shipping charges.

Under the export laws here, I will not be permitted to send a draft for the dog until it has arrived in South Africa. But I presume this will be only a technicality, so far as you are concerned. Or, if you doubt my honour, I am the South African representative of Torso Motors in Detroit, and it can vouch for my integrity.

I am sending along two copies of the veterinary permit. Looking forward anxiously to the dog's arrival, I am

Your Obliging Servant
Wilfrid MacKenzie

Pittsburgh, Pa.
July 3, 1952

Dear Riddle:

If your friend in South Africa thinks I am crazy enough to have the papers on Queenie transferred to a Canadian owner, ship the dog to Canada, and then have the Canadian transfer ownership to a South African who, for all I know, might be a tribal warrior with nothing but a spear for money, and all without me having a dime, he is crazy. In fact, as crazy as I think you are. Absolutely nothing doing.

Anyway, the vet says he will bet $6 Queenie is not pregnant.

Sincerely,
Mulvey

Telephone Call

July 5, 1952

Operator: Go ahead Mr. Riddle. I have Torso Motors for you.

Riddle: Is this the export division of Torso Motors?

Torso Motors: Yes, it is. This is Jones speaking. I am head of the division. What can I do for you?

Riddle: It is my understanding you have a representative in Potchefstroom, South Africa, named Wilfrid MacKenzie. Is that right?

Jones: Yes. He's our oldest foreign representative. A very fine man. But why do you ask?

(There follows 10 minutes of explanations. Then:)

Riddle: Would you be willing to pay the American owner for the dog, and then wait to receive reimbursement from the Canadian?

Jones: Well, this is all very sudden, and we don't know anything about the dog business. But if MacKenzie says it's okay, I guess we'd be willing to take the risk. But who is to guarantee that the Canadian will be honest?

Riddle: I don't think there is any worry there. She is a long time personal friend. And besides, the Canadian Kennel Club recommended her.

112

Jones: Well then, send me the details, and I'll send a check to this Mulvey fellow when you give the word.

Telephone Call

July 6, 1952

Operator: I have the cargo division of Pan American Airways for you.

Riddle: This is Maxwell Riddle in Cleveland. Do you have authorization from South Africa to ship a pregnant Boxer female about July 20?

Pan-Am: Yes, we do. But our information is that the dog will be coming from Canada.

Riddle: That's true, but I am in charge of arrangements.

Pan Am: Well, there will be no trouble. Live animals are given cargo preference. And certainly a pregnant one would be. But you'll have to have a waterproof crate. We approve the Tuttle Crate for this purpose.

Riddle: Where do you purchase a Tuttle crate?

Pan-Am: The only place they are sold is in Los Angeles, Cal. Let's see, now. For a Boxer, the size you'll need—the crate will cost $58.50. Plus shipping costs, of course.

TELEGRAM

July 7, 1952

McKee Industries
Los Angeles Airport
Los Angeles, Cal.
    Wiring $58.50 for crate Please ship air express collect to Frank Mulvey, Truncheon Kennels, Pittsburgh, Pa.
                    Maxwell Riddle
                    Cleveland Press

Pittsburgh, Pa.
July 11, 1952

Dear Riddle:

In all this excitement, I forgot about getting the owner of Ch. Warbird of Azuza to sign the American Kennel Club forms for registration of the litter. He has to attest to the mating. Well, you know, the dog was here in Pittsburgh with a professional handler, and it was the handler that allowed the mating to take place.

Anyway, I sent the AKC form to him at his home in Azuza, Cal. But his wife returned the papers, saying he is with the Armed Forces in Korea. So what do you suggest?

Sincerely,
Frank Mulvey

TELEGRAM

July 12, 1952

Frank Mulvey
Truncheon Kennels
Pittsburgh, Pa.

Send papers to his wife, with instructions to forward them to him in Korea for signing. Of course if you haven't paid the stud fee, he may not be eager to sign. So suggest you send it. Make check out to him, not his wife.

Riddle

Potchefstroom, Transvaal
Union of South Africa
5 July, 1952

Dear Mr. Riddle:

I forgot to send the veterinary permit in my last letter. I do so now. It sounds rough. But I think it is just a matter of red tape. I know the examining officer at Palmeifontein Airdrome, and I don't anticipate any trouble. However, you seem able to solve most difficulties.

Please don't, under any circumstances, give any indication that the bitch is pregnant. My permit covers a bitch only, and they might object to a bitch and a litter, even if the litter hasn't been born yet.

I don't think I'll even attempt to register the litter here until the pups are six months old. Because by that time with her being here six months already, she and the pups could stay in any case.

Your Humble Servant
Wilfrid MacKenzie

Veterinary Permit

The Veterinary Department of the Transvaal Division, Union of South Africa, hereby grants permission to Wilfrid MacKenzie of Potchefstroom, to import one Boxer bitch from the Province of Ontario, Canada, subject to the following conditions.

(a)   The dog is accompanied by a statement made under oath, and duly attested, that it has been in the possession of the Ontario owner continuously for a period of six months.

(b)   A statement from the veterinary officer in charge of the Ontario Government that there has been no case of canine rabies in Ontario for a period of one year past.

(c)   That sworn statements shall be made by the pilots of all airplanes upon which the dog travels, that it has not been out of its crate at any time during the trip, unless taken to a veterinary hospital.

Cleveland, Ohio
July 12, 1952

Dear Mrs. Burns:

I finally got the veterinary permit from MacKenzie. It is a killer, and we have been misled. Or perhaps, the South African government figured we were going to try to mislead it. Anyway, we will not be able to ship the dog unless I can figure an angle.

I have talked to Mr. Mulvey, and he is unwilling to do so, too. That is, to ship the dog. However, he says that Queenie has been in his kennel since birth, which is 16 months ago. She has never been out of it, except to go to four dog shows.

Also, Mulvey says that his veterinarian has made regular weekly checks of all the dogs in his kennel for several years. So now I have worked out a statement which this veterinarian will sign.

It will state that this dog has been under weekly veterinary examination since its birth 16 months ago; that it has never been exposed to rabies; and that it has been vaccinated against distemper, hepatitis, leptospirosis, and rabies; and that it is free from all these diseases.

Armed with this sworn statement, perhaps you can get your veterinarian to issue a sworn to, but weazel worded statement, such as this:

"This is to certify that this Boxer female, Juniper Queen, has been under continuous weekly veterinary inspection for the 16 months of her birth; that she is free of any communicable disease; and that he has been vaccinated against distemper, hepatitis, leptospirosis, and rabies."

This isn't exactly what we're ordered to supply. But the South Africans are mainly interested in preventing rabies in South Africa. And this statement, which will be true, in so far as it goes guarantees that. Besides, the examining officer ought to be willing to stretch a point rather than to send the dog all the way back from Africa.

I called the chief veterinary officer in Toronto. Upon your request, he will issue a statement that there has been no rabies in Ontario for a year.

116

The big obstacle here, at the moment, is that Mulvey's vet still says the dog is not pregnant.

Sincerely,
Maxwell Riddle

TELEGRAM
July 15, 1952

Maxwell Riddle
Cleveland Press
Cleveland Ohio
Two vets here say Queenie definitely pregnant. Have signed papers and have sent them to Mrs. Burns, When do I get paid?
Mulvey

Telephone Call

July 15, 1952

Operator: Go ahead, Mr. Riddle. I have Mr. Jones of Torso Motors for you.

Riddle: Mr. Jones?

Jones: Yes. This is Jones.

Riddle: This is Maxwell Riddle at the Cleveland Press. Have you heard from MacKenzie?

Jones: Yes. And he has okayed the plan. We'll pay off. How much is it, and who do we make the check out to?

Riddle: Well, the cost of the dog is $475, and the air express on the crate was $17.50, which Mulvey, the owner of the dog has paid. So make the check Frank Mulvey, and include both amounts. Mulvey has got so interested in this affair that he'll donate the cost of shipment of the dog to Buffalo. I paid for the crate. So send me a check for $58.50.

117

Telephone Call

July 18, 1952

Operator: Here is your party, Mr. Mulvey.
Mulvey: Is that you, Riddle?
Riddle: Yes. Is everything all right with your pregnant damsel?
Mulvey: Yes, she's showing those pups already. Now I'm in trouble though. Mrs. Burns sent back the transfer papers on the bitch. They have to go to the American Kennel Club, which will issue new papers, and an export certificate made out to her. But, you know how it is. It will take weeks to get those papers through, and we haven't got weeks to spend.
Riddle: Well, you send the papers special delivery to the American Kennel Club, and mark them for the attention of George Lowe. I'll call him up and ask him if he can put them through personally, the day they arrive.

Telephone Call

July 18, 1952

Operator: I have the American Kennel Club for you, Mr. Riddle.
Riddle: Mr. Lowe?
Lowe: Yes. Riddle? How are you?
(Follows five minutes of explanation)
Lowe: Then all we have to do is to transfer the papers to Mrs. Burns?
Riddle: Yes, that's all.
Lowe: Well, I see nothing wrong with that, provided the papers are in order. I'll try to handle it for you immediately when they arrive.

118

New York, N.Y.
July 19, 1952

Mr. Frank Mulvey
Truncheon Kennels
Pittsburgh, Pa.
Dear Mr. Mulvey:

Just a note to advise you that today we are sending to Winnifred Burns, Registration Certificate covering the Boxer "Hofbrau's Juniper Queen"—No. W-259284, showing the dog in the recorded ownership of Winnifred Burns.

Sincerely,
George Lowe
Executive Secy.
American Kennel Club

Welland, Ont.
July 20, 1952

Dear Max:

The papers on Queenie arrived this morning. I immediately called Harry Hubertson at Ottawa, and explained to him I had a bred bitch, and I needed to get the papers transferred to my name immediately. He said if I'd send the papers special delivery-airmail to Ottawa, he'd order the transfer the same day.

Then I checked with the customs sergeant. He said he'd require a customs receipt to go on the dog, since it must be shipped back to New York to catch Pan American. That is no good. Because the dog would then arrive in South Africa with a customs receipt showing it had entered Canada just before shipment. So we'll have to work out that detail.

I also called Trans Canada Air Lines. They said they could handle the dog, and would deliver it to Pan American. They'd like a few days notice, of course.

Now for the best news. My veterinarian has studied your letter. In view of the certificates you are sending along, he will issue the sort of oath you suggested. I have talked with my attorney. He says it will be a little "weazle worded," to borrow

119

your own expression. He says it won't conform to what the South Africans demand. But that, in view of their desire only to keep rabies out of the country, they might pass it. So my conscience is clear.

Sincerely,
Winnie Burns

Telephone Call

July 21, 1952

Operator: I have Welland, Ontario, for you. Go ahead.

Riddle: Winnie. Mrs. Burns?

Mrs. Burns: Yes. This is Winnie. Is that you Max?

Riddle: Yes. We shipped the dog this morning. She'll arrive on the New York Central at Buffalo at 4 p.m. today. If you go over and get her today, you'll have time to get the certificates from your own veterinarian. The Pan American plane leaves New York Thursday morning. That means you'll have to get Queenie aboard the Trans Canada plane at 4 p.m. Wednesday. That is, the day after tomorrow. Both Trans Canada and Pan American go into Idlewild International Airport, so there shouldn't be any delay in transfer. Queenie ought to arrive at Palmeifontein Airport Saturday night, if all goes well. I'll cable MacKenzie to expect her.

Mrs. Burns: We're ready here. I'll go over to Buffalo, and Bob Harrison and I will meet Queenie at the train. The customs people know both Bob and me, because we're always taking dogs back and forth across the border to the shows. So we shouldn't have too much trouble. We'll figure out some way to escape that customs receipt deal.

120

Welland, Ont.
July 24, 1952

Dear Max:

Well, we got the little girl safely off yesterday afternoon, and the service we got was wonderful. I recalled that a friend of ours in Toronto knew the airport manager, and all I had to do was mention his name. They practically rolled out the red carpet.

He insisted on wiring Pan American that the dog was coming, and I didn't dissuade him, although I knew you had arrangements all made.

At the last moment, the chief registrar at the Canadian National Live Stock Records, Harry Hubertson, gave me a statement that the dog was registered in Canada, including a registration number for her, even though the papers weren't completely processed. The lawyer added this to the affidavit, so everything would be in order in South Africa.

But we ran into a snag which is going to cost someone $7.50. We couldn't get the dog and the crate both in the car. So I just took the dog across in the car, and said it was mine, and we got by without a customs receipt on the dog, which was wonderful, and what we wanted.

But then, when we tried to bring the crate in, we got stopped. Bob did a lot of fibbing around, but we couldn't get by. But it turned out that Bob and the customs officer are lodge brothers. So the officer valued the crate at $25, and we only paid $7.50 duty. Which isn't bad, considering.

I followed your advice, and put cans of Canadian packed dog food in the crate. So this, too, will make it look as though she was coming from Canada. I put in enough to last five days. I'll donate the dog food. But I do want back that $7.50.

Such an interesting experience!

Sincerely,
Mrs. Winnifred Burns

Telephone Call

July 25, 1952

Operator: Mrs. Burns, I have your call to Mr. Riddle in Cleveland.

Mrs. Burns: Max, this is Winnie. We have troubles. Trans Canada called this morning and said that Pan American had refused to take the dog. Said it couldn't handle her for three weeks. Something about getting behind because of the steel strike, and having a shipment of horses to go first, or something.

Trans Canada has the dog in a veterinary hospital. You know, she looks to me like she'll bust out all over with pups any minute now. So TCA says it has made temporary arrangements with Sabena Belgian to take her, if we'll approve.

Riddle: Okay, nothing else we can do. When will Sabena ship her out?

Mrs. Burns: The TCA man said Saturday morning.

Riddle: Well,that won't be so bad. Tell them to go ahead. It's better than Queenie having pups in Idlewild Airport. And, in the meantime, I'll check with Sabena.

Telephone Call

Saturday, July 26, 1952

Operator: Here is your New York call.

Riddle: Is this the cargo department of Sabena Belgian?

Sabena: Yes, it is.

Riddle: Do you have a Boxer dog there, brought in from Toronto for shipment to South Africa?

Sabena: Yes, we do. That is, the dog is in a veterinary hospital in the possession of Trans Canada.

122

Riddle:	I was informed you would ship her this morning.
Sabena:	Yes, we had intended to do so. But the crate was so big we couldn't get it through the door of the plane. That plane is a DC-4. We have a DC-6 leaving tomorrow, and we'll put the dog aboard it. But there is one hitch.
Riddle:	What's that?
Sabena:	Our rules require payment in advance when live animals are shipped so far.
Riddle:	But Transvaal Cartage Ltd. of Johannesburg has guaranteed payment at that end.
Sabena:	Yes, we know that. But ours are house rules laid down in Brussels. We can't change them here, even though we were notified of the guaranteed payment by Trans Canada. But, if you get payment guaranteed here, we could stretch a point.
Riddle:	How? What do you mean?
Sabena:	If we have a responsible guarantor in this country, we could ship the dog, and bill the company or person.
Riddle:	But this is Saturday. How can I get that done today?
Sabena:	It's an interesting question, but your problem.

Telephone Call

Saturday, July 26, 1952

Operator:	Mr. Riddle, I have Torso Motors for you.
Riddle:	I'd like to speak to Mr. Jones in the export division.
Torso Motors:	He's not here on Saturdays. In fact, that department is closed for the day.
Riddle:	Can you give me his home phone number?
Torso Motors:	Well, that's very irregular . . .
Riddle:	This is an emergency, and it doesn't concern company business.
Torso Motors:	Well, in that case . . .

123

Telephone Call
Sunday, July 27, 1952

Operator: I have the cargo department of Sabena Belgian for you, Mr. Riddle. Go ahead.

Riddle: This is Maxwell Riddle, speaking from Cleveland. Did you get authorization from Torso Motors to bill them for the shipping costs for that Boxer dog which is going to South Africa?

Sabena: Yes, we did. That part is all taken care of now.

Riddle: Did you ship the dog?

Sabena: Well, no we didn't. She's still in the custody of Trans Canada. But she's at a veterinary hospital, and is doing all right. We plan to ship her some day next week. But, if you'll pardon my language, how the Hell is it, a Clevelander is so interested in the shipment of a Canadian dog going from Toronto to Joburg? And how is it that a Detroit firm will pay the costs?

Riddle: Well, it's a business matter. But what is more important, do you want that dog to have pups in your airplane?

Sabena: What? What did you say?

Riddle: I said that bitch is pregnant, and if you don't get her to Johannesburg within the next six days, she'll have pups right in your airplane. Who'll be responsible then?

(Sounds of choking at the New York end)

Sabena: Why we didn't know. We had no idea . . . We haven't seen the dog, you know. Well, rest assured we'll get after this matter right away.

CABLEGRAM

Potchefstroom, Transvaal July 27, 1952.
Maxwell Riddle
Cleveland Press
Cleveland, Ohio
Why the holdup. Stop. Received cable dog
not coming Pan American but Sabena. Stop. Not
on Sabena. Have arranged immediate ship-
ment British Overseas Airways. Advise return
cable arrival time.
MacKenzie

CABLEGRAM

Wilfrid MacKenzie
Potchefstroom Transvaal
Union of South Africa
Dog shipped this morning. Pilots and
stewardesses instructed give special atten-
tion. Dog being fed special foods and vitamin
mineral tablets in diet and instructions
from Mrs. Burns. Should arrive via Sabena
Wednesday night or Thursday morning.
Riddle

CABLEGRAM
Munsan, Korea
(via Army Radio Communication Service)
July 30
Maxwell Riddle
Cleveland Press
Cleveland, Ohio
Registration papers for mating and puppies signed under oath here. With oath of handler who made mating, should satisfy South Africa Kennel Club.

Major Norbert Leary
Azuza Kennels

Welland, Ontario
July 30.

Dear Max:

Well, I suppose the little lady got there safely after all this trouble. I forgot to tell you that, through a quirk in the rules here, Mr. MacKenzie will be listed as the breeder of the pups, and not, as in your country, the owner of the bitch at the time of mating.

Of course, the South African Kennel Club may have other ideas on this. But we've done the best we could. This was fun once, but I don't know that I'd want to do it again. Anyway though, I now know all the tricks of the trade.

Sincerely,
Winnifred Burns

CABLEGRAM
Johannesburg, South Africa July 31), 1952.
Maxwell Riddle
Cleveland Press
Cleveland, Ohio

Queenie arrived safely. Definitely in whelp.

MacKenzie

Potchefstroom, Transvaal
Union of South Africa
Aug. 8, 1952

Dear Mr. Riddle:

I delayed writing until I had the full story, and we are—all of us—absolutely delighted, both with "Queenie" and her beautifully marked litter of seven puppies.

We guess Queenie didn't stand the long trip very well, as she arrived kind of thin and with her back roached, and you could nearly count her puppies. She wagged her tail when I took her out of her beautiful crate, and we fed her at the road-house outside the airdrome—just enough to settle her gnawing hunger. We let her sleep by our bed, and in three days, she looked like a different dog.

I sat up from 1 a.m. to 6 a.m. on the 6th, and kept her pups warm with a hot water bottle, as it is winter here. I really got a thrill as each beautifully marked puppy arrived.

We think you are a wizard, as you must have had some trouble working this all out. We are going to name one of these puppies MacKenzie's Maxwell Riddle. So you will leave your permanent stamp on Boxers in South Africa.

You know, I had to laugh. The plane bringing Queenie was two hours late. So I plied the veterinarian with Scotch. And by the time Queenie arrived, he was in good shape.

"Looks a little pregnant, doesn't she?" he said.

I told him I supposed everyone had been stuffing her on the trip. He just sort of smiled. Then he looked at the export permit, and all the affidavits, and kept saying "hum," "hum." That's all he said, but he signed the papers letting her in.

You know, two days later, the veterinary surgeon for Transvaal called and wanted to pick up my permit to import a dog from Ontario. He said a rabies case had been reported there. So he was going to revoke my permit. But when I told him the dog was already here, he seemed satisfied.

Well, thanks old man. I'm sending you a lion skin purse for your wife, and a leopard skin bill fold and ivory cigarette holder for yourself.

Your Obliging Servant
Wilfrid MacKenzie

Note: In due course, the gifts arrived. My wife adores the lion skin handbag. But the leopard skin bill fold does not fit American money. And I don't smoke. More important, MacKenzie forgot to mark "unsolicited gift" in the package. So the customs people socked me $26 duty on the items.

Second Note: All the puppies, and their mother, Queenie, won South African championships.

Final Note: It's nice to know that I'm at stud, to approved bitches only, in the Union of South Africa.

10

The Innocent Dog Judge Abroad

While in Nairobi I told the kind Pekingese lady introduced in an earlier chapter that I wanted to meet Dr. Leakey. Dr. Lewis Leakey is the world famous anthropologist who discovered the earliest human-type skulls at Olduvai.

"That's impossible," she said. "You must have an appointment two months in advance."

The next night, a Wirehaired Fox Terrier breeder had a cocktail party and dinner for me. This was during the height of the Mau Mau terror. A pick-up truck drove up as we talked on the lawn. A man in civilian clothes was driving while a man in the bed of the truck manned a machine gun.

"Who in the world is that?" I asked.

"That is Dr. Leakey. He has come to see you."

Indeed he had. It turned out that among his startling list of accomplishments was being a dog judge. And further, he was a Dalmatian breeder who was, at that time, trying to breed long coated Dalmatians as a protection against mosquitos. The next day he invited me to the Corinden Museum, which he had founded, and of which he was the head. I had to pass by three stations of armed guards, and Dr. Leakey himself had an armed revolver on his desk.

Earlier, in the old Belgian Congo, officials has sent me back country to a village where I might see some Basenji dogs. But they had issued a strict warning to me.

"Do not use the word Basenji. It means 'savage' in their language. And if you use the word, the natives might think you are calling *them* savages. And you could get a spear in the back. We call them Saba Dogs, meaning, 'Dogs of the Queen of Sheba.'"

Now Dr. Leakey also jumped on me for the use of the word Basenji. It seems that he had at one time scoured the back country for purebred Basenjis for export to Great Britain. Dr. Leakey gave a name for the breed which, translated, means "Dog of the Forest." But others have called it the Congo Dog, or the Congo Bush Dog. In some areas it has also been called "the Jumping Up And Down Dog." Dr. Leakey assured me that the only purebred Basenji in Africa was owned by a colonel who lived at Arusha in Tanganyika. So I went there.

But before leaving Nairobi, I was taken to a fancy hotel night club where I was introduced to some dinner guests, who were told that I was from Cleveland in the United States.

"Wonderful," a lady said. "Perhaps you can tell us the very latest on the Sam Sheppard murder case."

Another said: "I suppose that you people think we have lions roaming the streets."

I assured her that we did not. I was staying at that time at a converted game lodge. Just at daylight I heard a terrible commotion in the street. I looked out the window, and so help me, a lioness was majestically walking down the middle of the street, totally ignoring the frantic barking of a dozen dogs.

The next morning there was a similar uproar. This time I ventured out to determine the cause. A large python had got into a chicken house, had swelled its belly with a number of chickens, and now was stuck in a drain pipe. A dozen men were dragging it out.

The only hotel at Arusha had a sign on the door: "No dogs allowed!" This always irritates me. But as I entered there was a very beautiful German Shepherd wandering about the lobby. I inquired about this.

"Oh, that is the owner's dog. Naturally he is allowed in."

I asked where I might meet the colonel with the Basenji.

"He lives far out in the national game park," was the answer. "You know, he is in charge of it. But his secretary is in the dining room having dinner. You can recognize her because she has her Pekingese dog with her."

Sure enough, there was the lady, Pekingese in her lap, sharing food together. Later, in the coffee lounge, we talked. Her husband had been a veterinarian in Tanganyika for 28 years. He had bought a cattle farm. One night, his farm help reported that a band of nomadic Masai were moving through the farm, and were taking his cattle along. The veterinarian got his machine gun, took along a helper, jumped in his Land Rover, and pursued the Masai. He proceeded to disarm them. All but one. That one speared him in the back.

British troops rounded up the Masai and held them on a

131

murder charge. But the judge ruled it to be justifiable homicide. "He had lived in Tanganyika long enough to know that the two greatest disgraces a Masai warrior can suffer are to be seen naked and without his weapons."

"What has become of British justice?" mourned the murdered veterinarian's wife.

The next morning, the colonel agreed to take me to his home for lunch. He had no way to notify his wife that he would be bringing a guest for lunch. We arrived in his big Mercedes Benz, had cocktails and a six course lunch. His wife was about half his age and very beautiful.

During lunch, she said: "I am convinced that the white man must leave Africa. I don't know which will be first, and which will be last, but leave they must." The colonel knew that she was talking to an American newspaper reporter, but he did not stop her.

Ah, the dog. It truly deserved the name Basenji. A German Shepherd had torn a great hole in her side. She was too savage to permit it to be sewed up. So the colonel contented himself with throwing an antiseptic powder into the wound from a distance.

Ceylon Assignment

Ceylon, or as it is now known, Sri Lanka, has a thousand miles of beautiful beaches. I was swimming at one of these when a Singhalese gentleman, swimming with flippers, swam out to me.

"I say, aren't you the American dog judge?"

"Yes."

"Well, then, we are having a beauty contest on the beach near the hotel this afternoon. We would be honored if you would consent to judge it."

I agreed instantly. I had visions of dozens of beautiful women in bikinis—English, Portuguese, Singhalese, and maybe even Tamil. But not one of the girls who took part was wearing even a modest swim suit. Without exception, they were wrapped from toe to chin in flowing robes.

It is also unfortunate that at a beauty contest of this type, you cannot feel the brisket, or even the stifles of the contestants.

Fig Leaves

It was in Ceylon, too, that Frederick Obeyesekere, a Cambridge boxing champion and the head of the dog show, told me of the visit of the English duchess to his titled uncle. In Ceylon, the children of the lower classes run naked until about two years of age. Then they are fitted with a G-string, to which is attached a metal fig leaf.

Just before the age of puberty, the children are fully clothed. This means that the boys must wear the equivalent of trousers, and the girls must be covered from chin to feet. I have watched women bathing in a tank (a Singhalese word for reservoir). People bathed and washed their clothes in these tanks even though they later got their drinking water from them.

The women would modestly make certain adjustments to their underclothes, shimmy out of them without disturbing the outer garment, and then wade into the water. They would then soap themselves while keeping on the outer garment.

So back to the English duchess. She was at lunch on the last day of her visit.

"Sir Richard," she said, "I have bought many things in Ceylon which I treasure. But one thing which I could not buy, and would like very much to have, is one of those little metal fig leaves which the children wear."

Sir Richard summoned his house boys.

"The English lady wishes to take home a fig leaf. She must leave here in one hour. Please get one for her."

Three quarters of an hour later, the house boys returned, and the No. 1 House boy reported sadly:

"Your honor, we have searched the district carefully. But we have been unable to find one which would fit the English lady."

Purely Personal—Japanese Adventure

I was the first licensed American judge to officiate at a dog show in Japan. The trip included going out on a hunting party on the last day of the Japanese hunting season. I was ill-prepared for this, since I had come from warm Hawaii, and was headed for Hong Kong and Ceylon. It was the spring of 1959. The cherry blossom season was nearly over, but the weather was unusually cold for the Tokyo area.

Three television stations and a radio station or two covered the dog show. I was quoted around the world, and particularly on my comments on the Akita, Shiba, and other Japanese dogs which, I felt, should do well in America. Five Japanese judges, an interpreter, and a stenographer followed me about.

It is not hard to imagine the fear and trepidation I felt at judging the Akitas and Shibas. I had seen only two Akitas and no Shibas. But I had studied hard, and the dogs seemed to fall into place. When I had picked my best Akita, everyone bowed. It was their grand champion.

It was different when they showed me their grand champion Great Dane. He was a beautiful animal which they called a harlequin. But he was black except for white legs, feet, and belly. And I had to tell them that he would be disqualified at most shows in the world. Of course, he had been sold to them by an American.

That night there was a grand dinner party. Everyone wore a shield, including me, on their lapels. At the top were the Japanese and American flags, and beneath that "In Memoriam." I asked the meaning of this and got the following information.

"There are five warring clubs here, and no one from one club would show at the show of another, and no one would ever dream of attending a dinner given by another club. But at this, the 'Well Come Maxwell Riddle Dog Show' sponsored by the magazine Friend of Dogs, members of all five clubs have turned out."

I was domiciled at the Imperial Hotel where, because of the publicity, my father's long time hunting and fishing com-

135

panion, Wah King Thom of Honolulu, was able to find me. He had been tiger hunting in India.

I was loaned boots too large for me and a heavy rain coat, and we set off for the day's hunt on the slopes of Mt. Fujiyama within sight of the emperor's own hunting territory. My particular companion had a one shot 10 gauge hammer shot gun, which he sometimes swung toward my belly. He had two dogs, an American Foxhound and a Pointer. We hunted in a deep ravine, the walls of which were too steep to climb.

The man had a great system. The Pointer would climb up the side of the ravine and come to a point on a pheasant. The Foxhound would then rush up and flush the pheasant or perhaps a Japanese quail. Since the birds could not fly straight up, they flew down, thus making the most difficult of all shots. We didn't hit many.

It rained all that day. Toward evening we went to a Japanese restaurant on the second floor of the building. All had to take off their shoes and leave them at the bottom of the stairs. We sat around the floor of a square room. I do not smell well, but I believe the odor was what one would call all pervasive from 44 pairs of feet, all soaked in sweat and perhaps rain.

An earthen mug of hot sake was placed before each person. The interpreter explained to me that if a person wanted to honor me, he would bring his jug of sake, kneel before me, and pour a drink for me. I must then return the favor by pouring him a drink from my jug.

Each person wanted to honor me thus. For them, it was one drink; for me, 43. So I was sitting there absolutely paralyzed, and with my head about to explode, when the interpreter leaned over and spoke very earnestly.

"Mr. Riddle, we did not know what kind of a man you were, so we wrote to a man in Honolulu who knows you. He replied: 'Do not worry about Mr. Riddle. He is a very strong and virile man.' Mr. Riddle, we thought he meant with the Geisha girls, but now we know it was with the sake."

Dinner was a ten course affair, served with quarts of beer. A young lady was assigned to help me with the chop sticks, and she was particularly valuable when I was served a large fish head. She delicately extracted the eyes and popped them into my mouth. I managed to wash them down with beer, whereupon that many swallows of beer were quickly replenished by solicitous waitresses.

All the while my host kept telling me not to eat too much because afterward we were going over the mountain to his home at the resort town of Atami. And there, he said, "We will have a real feast."

On the way over, the car windows were kept open. I nearly froze, but sobered up. My host's house at Atami was on the mountain side. Once inside the house, we took off our shoes. There was a long, broad flight of stairs, and the servants were at the top, bowing their welcome.

"Take off your clothes," the interpreter said. He was, by the way, a good dog man, raised in California, and caught in Japan by the war. He had remained there. And as it happened, I had known him earlier. He had joined the party at my host's house.

"You don't have to be afraid to take off your clothes before the servants in Japan," he said. "We are going to take a hot bath." I was wearing light nylon underclothes which I could wash out at night on the long journey. And I was freezing. All the others were wearing long, thermal underwear.

Then came the task of fitting me with a proper length heavy damask kimono. Oh, the goose flesh! The huge bath tub was filled from a hot spring which was piped into the house. It was covered with boards, which the servants of the bath removed. The water was too hot to enter. But in any case, you wash yourself first. So the ladies dumped pails of water on us, we soaped, and then had more pails of water dumped on us.

"Bring your towel," said the interpreter, Kameo.

"But what will I use to dry myself?" I objected.

"In Japan, you use a wet towel."

I began to believe that I would never reach Hong Kong alive. After soaking in the tub, I dried myself with the wet towel, which I wrung out as well as I could, put on my nylon undershirt and briefs, and then that heavy kimono. Kameo put on his long thermal underwear and kimono. Then we went into the next room while the others got into the tub.

The only heat came from charcoal in what had once been a grease tub. We had another feast. This time three Geisha came to entertain us. My host instructed Kameo to explain to me that these were among the few true Geisha left in Japan. That is, they were graduates of the royal school at Kyoto, and had been given their diplomas in the presence of the emperor himself.

One was about 60. She played the three stringed samisen, the lute of Japan which has a five note octave, and is used to accompany poetic and musical recitals. A 40 year-old Geisha sang, and a girl of 21 or 22, danced the great classic dances of Japan.

The youngest one was quite lovely, and she also helped me with the chop sticks. My legs stuck out from the knee down, and my elbows to my finger tips, from the kimono. The girls found my hairy arms and legs quite fascinating, and each pulled the hairs quite seriously.

The food, and what must have been a barrel of hot sake, made the party quite gay. Finally, the dancer had Kameo tell me that she could dance the "western" dances. Since I was still freezing, I was happy to oblige. So there we were in stocking feet, dancing American-style to the wailing of the singer, and the alien music of the samisen. I began to hope that my host would put me to bed with the girl, if only to keep me warm.

But at a certain signal, which I did not see, the three Geisha disappeared, a wall was pushed back, and there were two bedding mats placed before the family altar. They were like sleeping bags. Kameo, at five feet two, filled his nicely. The pillow was a block of wood. I stuck out from nipples upward, and I could not use the wooden pillow. Kameo, however, put it under his neck and fell asleep instantly.

In the morning, a servant pushed back a wall, and there was the garden, with a pond covered by a thin coating of ice. We are going to take another bath, I was told, whereupon I began again to fear for my life. Later that morning I was put on the train for Kyoto, without an interpreter, and with a sack of quail to be delivered to someone who would meet me in the immense Kyoto station. No one did, so I finally shoved the bag of quail into the hands of an old beggar.

138

I managed to get to the Myako Hotel and into a room in the old Japanese section. In those days, Kyoto had no English alphabet street signs, and the people in my section of the hotel spoke no English. But I managed to reach a missionary friend who took me about Kyoto for two days, showing me all the shrines and temples, and serving better than any tour guide could. We passed the Geisha Theatre, and I made a note of it.

Pleading fatigue that night, I left my friend, and managed to convey to the hotel desk clerk that I wanted a taxi to take me to the Geisha Theatre. I began to wander the streets in darkness. Eventually I came to a three letter word in English, the only Western alphabet I saw in those days at Kyoto. It was a small, lighted window sign "BAR."

I went in. It was a small cubby hole type, with one booth and five stools around the bar itself. There were three girls, a man and the bar tender. They were playing an aged wind up Victrola, and Western music. They seemed very surprised to see a white man. After some gesturing, I got it across that I wanted a shot of Johnnie Walker whiskey. I sat in the booth to drink it.

There was a conference at the bar. The Victrola was cranked up, and the girls and man got in front of my booth. The music was an instrumental version of Suwannee River. The four knew the words to the first line, then hummed the rest. I bought a drink all around. There followed Old Black Joe. I bought another round.

About the third round, two wandering musicians came in. One, with a guitar, had an Elvis Presley haircut. The other, shorter and heavier, had the heavily veined nose which alcoholics sometimes get and which reminded me of the expression "sunburned through a sieve." He had a trumpet which, so help me, had been patched in at least four places with black plumber's tape. The guitarist took the rain shield from his guitar, the trumpeter struck up, and the two played Love Me Truly. I bought another round.

Two more musicians wandered in. The first pair did not like this, but I was buying the drinks. The party was getting lively. The girls were drinking beer, and I noted they would disappear after consuming a quart. I finally realized they were going to the lavatory and throwing up so as to be able to drink more without getting drunk.

Then an older man came in. He spoke English, said he had been in America, and had been a voice teacher in Italy. One of the girls, he said, was one of his pupils, and he added that alcohol was bad for the voice. I bought a couple more rounds of drinks.

Finally, I announced that I had to leave, but that I had no idea where I was, nor how to get back to the hotel. There was a conference. The voice teacher bought a round of drinks. Then the bar tender closed the bar. The whole group then escorted me to the head of the street where I could wait for a taxi. The trumpets blared, the group sang, windows opened, and choice Japanese swear words rang out.

Then, just as a taxi was pulling up, the trumpets blared "Goodnight Sweetheart." And why not? I had certainly been the angel of that party. I got back to the Myako, went to my room and took off my shoes in the alcove. The bed mat was laid out on the floor, a night lamp beside it, and a soft Western style pillow. I laughed myself to sleep.

The next morning my missionary friend picked me up and took me to the train. I had an assigned window seat with a Canadian next to me. My friend stood by the window and waved goodbye.

"That your girl friend?" he asked.

"No. A missionary from my home town. She has taken me to the shrines about Kyoto."

A dining car attendant came through, and we ordered lunch. When it was ready, and a table was vacant, we were summoned. Across from us was a brassy, brazen-voiced Englishman who represented American Express on a Swedish cruise ship. The fourth man, whom I suspected might be a missionary, kept quiet.

"How long have you been in Japan?" asked the Canadian.

"Two weeks," I replied.

"Have you had a girl yet?"

"No," I replied.

"I have," he said. "Every night. Well, I'm 73, so I have missed a night or two. But I told my travel agent that I wanted to be in a hotel where I could have a girl every night. He put me in the Imperial. So I checked with the desk clerk, and he said 'no girl.' So I raised hell with the local travel bureau agent and he put me in a hotel where I could get a girl. But what is the matter with you?"

"Well," I said, trying to be humorous about it, "I came up from Africa to Paris, and all the famed houses of ill-fame had been closed by the police. And now I arrive in Japan and find that the ancient profession has been outlawed here, too. So I guess ill fortune is just preceding me."

"It's a hell of a situation," said the American Express agent, who could be heard over the entire dining car. "And you can just blame Eleanor Roosevelt for that. She's the one who is responsible."

I never found out why. And the fourth man just smiled, got a little red in the face, and looked down at his food.

Brazilian Incidents

After having judged a weekend dog show at Rio de Janeiro, I was invited to a party at an estate far up the mountainside. The then president of the Brazil Kennel Club took me up the mountain an hour and a half earlier than the stated hour of the party because she wanted to show me the estate, which overlooked the city far below.

As in many areas in the more tropical areas of Brazil, the house was in three sections, separated by breezeways. Thus, the kitchen was in one section, so that neither kitchen smells nor heat could spread into the other sections. The middle section, which had very high ceilings, contained the dining and living rooms. The bedrooms were in the third section.

From the home one could look down upon a paddock, arranged in a half circle, and bounded by a dozen stables for the hosts' hunters, of which he was very proud. The house area was surrounded by a 12 foot high steel or iron picket fence. The gates were ponderous and opened wide.

We arrived to the furious barking of eight black dogs. They were half black American Cocker Spaniel and half black Labrador Retriever. We rang the bell, but for a time neither it nor the furious uproar of the dogs brought any result. Then we heard a woman screaming in both Portuguese and English. From the English, I could gather that she was swearing with the choicest of Portuguese epithets at a servant named Carlos. Then she arrived, along with Carlos. She was in a bath robe. She had been in her sauna. My escort had explained to me that she was Russian, but that she spoke fluent English and Portuguese as well. Her husband, a Czech, was reputed to speak seven languages.

The dogs were finally locked up, and then our still sputtering hostess explained to us that Carlos was the stupidest man in the world.

"His real name is Jesus," she said. "But I am a Christian. I just can't go around shouting at him 'Jesus Christ, you stupid son-of-a-bitch' so I changed his name to Carlos, and now I can swear at him without being blasphemous."

My host came about 6 p.m., as did a dozen other guests. He was a collector of Renaissance wood carvings and chests. The walls were hung with wooden angels from a dozen ancient European churches. A 12 foot high wooden chest against one wall, served as his well stocked liquor chest.

At one point during the evening the host had a groom saddle his favorite hunter, an importation from England. He was so proud of this animal that, in order the better to show if off, he rode it into the living room. The hostess swore mightily, not because of any damage to the parque floor but because of the prospect of "horse chocolates" on it.

Meanwhile someone had taken down an antique hunting horn from its place on the wall. This was being passed around for inspection, and various people were trying to blow it. The horn was of a type which my father had owned. I was then a Boy Scout troop bugler and had also learned to wind the hunting horn. So I gave it a mighty blast.

The startled horse leaped about four feet, landed partly in a chair, and threw mine host, who got a bloody nose and a black eye. All this to the rich invective of his wife.

When the party was over, a gentleman who must have been an Alpine racer driver, and who was now somewhat stoned, drove me down the mountain to my hotel in Rio.

Several days later I had an appointment to meet a Brazilian friend at the Jockey Club. He was late and, as I waited, my host of the party came along. I told him what a great time I had had at his party. This made him very happy.

"Come again on Sunday," he said. "We are going to have an informal party."

Recently, Dro John Maasley, one of our American Kennel Club field representatives, reminded me of an incident which happened at a show in his area. I had given a woman with bright red hair—and an immense amount of it—a group placing. She got so excited that, dragging the dog with one hand and brandishing the ribbon with the other, she rushed about the ring at what for her was high speed. The hair was a wig. First it skewed half over her face, and then fell off entirely.

It happened at a show at Belo Horizonte, the beautiful Brazilian city which was built entirely according to plan and served as a model for Brasilia. The show was on the grounds of a country club. Near the ring was a small pond. Across it was an arching walkway, or bridge, without guard rails. It was quite beautiful, and hundreds of people were drawn to walk over it.

A lady got best of breed with her Bulldog. She grabbed the ribbon and, screaming with delight, dragged the dog, who was somewhat unwilling, onto the arched bridge. The lady lost her balance, and both fell in. Oh, the screaming, the laughing, and the excitement as the lady and her dog were fished out! By the time the group was judged, the dog had dried off, but the lady, wet and bedraggled as she was, insisted on showing the dog. Could any gentleman judge have refused to give so gallant a dame the group first?

11

Joys(?) of Dog Judging

I once judged an entry of 12 Bernese Mountain Dogs. In those days the breed was comparatively rarer than today. The show was on a mountain top, the wind blew, and it rained. There was little space and I had to send the dogs out into the rain. A couple of breeds later, a Bernese exhibitor asked to talk to me.

"I have written out a formal complaint against you, and I am going to turn it in to the American Kennel Club. But I think that in fairness, I should let you read it first, and even give you a copy."

"Well, it is nice of you to tell me this, but what is your complaint?"

"I have the world's greatest Bernese Mountain Dog, and you have done it irreparable harm by placing it second in the class. You have just ruined its reputation, and I believe you should have to pay for this bad judging."

I thought a minute.

"But when I asked you to gait the dog, it lay down and put its feet up into the air."

"Yes, that is true. But I imported him from Switzerland, and the Swiss who know say he is the greatest Bernese Mountain Dog ever bred."

"Then when I tried to examine the dog, he lay down again, and you had a terrible time getting him back on his feet, didn't you?"

"Yes. But you are supposed to examine the structure and quality of the dog, and you didn't do that, at least not very well."

"But didn't the dog then get into a fight with other dogs? And, in spite of all that, didn't I give it second prize?"

"Yes, but he is the greatest dog in the world, and you have ruined his reputation."

"Well, then, I will be happy to escort you over to the superintendent and show chairman, and you can then file your complaint."

They convinced him that he should tear up the complaint. I do not know the further history of this super dog.

Questions of Alcohol

Oklahoma is supposedly a dry state, and it seems to have been completely so (legally speaking) at the time of this incident. The after-show party was held in the private downstairs dining room at a prominent restaurant. The tables were loaded with liquor bottles. Seeking to know the answer to this, I went around to the club president.

"I thought Oklahoma was dry."

"It is," he replied. "But I don't trust the bootleggers. So I have the sheriff go over to Texas and buy my liquor for me."

One of the best loved exhibitors in the Kansas-Texas-Oklahoma area was a Catholic priest. He was light hearted. He could be gay and funny, but he could also be deeply religious. At another Oklahoma show, at the after-show dinner, bottles appeared. The priest came to my table with a half gallon jug of whiskey.

"Will you have a little more holy water?" he said, filling my glass.

Repartee

The late Haskell Schuffman was judging Lhasa Apsos. After best of breed a lady came into the ring to give him a lecture.

"I don't know how you could have done this to my little girl. Judge So-and-So gave her winners two weeks ago, and Judge So-and-So gave her first and reserve at another show. And now you have given my baby fourth in the class."

She turned to leave the ring. But Haskell, in his deep booming voice, called her back. He shook his finger at her and said:

"Lady, I am not responsible for the mistakes of other judges."

Another judge told an irate exhibitor:

"You paid $9 to get my opinion. But I didn't pay a penny for yours and wouldn't give you a counterfeit penny for it. Now get out of my ring."

Still another judge tried to tell a loser the things which were wrong with her dog. But to every criticism, she said that everyone told her those were the best features of the dog. Finally, the judge began to get angry.

"Lady," he said, "Come back next week, and I'll think up something else to tell you."

I confess to being slow witted, particularly when repartee is required. Mostly, when I've tried, I've come close to getting a punch in the nose. But I did have one triumph. It was at a show with 100 degree temperature and humidity. The ring table was six feet long. Two Pekingese were in the class. After gaiting them I had their lady owners put them at opposite ends of the table. One lady was wearing a low cut dress and no brassiere. Thus when she bent over, her more than ample breasts all but fell out of her dress. I gave her first. When the two women had entered the ring, it was obvious that they were bitter enemies, and the temperature had gone up to 10 degrees more.

"I suppose," said the second place owner, "if I would wear a low cut dress and expose myself so shamelessly, I could win."

I took the two women by the elbows.

"Ladies," I said, "I belong to a nudist colony, and nothing either one of you two ladies could show me would change my mind."

Someone from the American Kennel Club was watching. I did not know him at the time. He came into the ring and asked what I had said to make those two women get so red faced. I told him. He wanted to be very formal and even tried to scowl to keep from laughing. Finally, he had an answer.

"True nudists never use the word 'colony,'" he said and walked away.

12

Dogs and Sex

And so, dear reader, we come to the last chapter, that one which deals with sex and dogs. It is, as we said in the beginning, that conversations about dogs always end up in discussions on feeding, or about sex. So did we start with the one, and we end with the other.

Dog people are neither more nor less moral than any other group. But they are less inhibited in their language, and they are far better educated in biology, animal and human than are most other people.

They are not unaware of the surprise and shock experienced by those just getting into the sport. And they often find the reactions of the newcomers to be uproariously funny.

And so may you find this final chapter by the craziest dogger of them all!

Dear Mr. Riddle:
I have a four months old Shetland Sheepdog. And sometimes he grabs my leg with his forepaws, and then begins pumping motions. I know what he wants, and I try to help him out. But isn't he a little young for this? And will it hurt him? Afterward he has such a satisfied look in his eyes.

Sincerely,
Mrs. Aberjo

Dear Mrs. Aberjo:
Puppies of both sexes do this. And to be very earthy about the matter, about the third or fourth days after birth, lambs try to mount their mothers. Unless you want much trouble and embarrassment later on, you must stop this habit of your pup. Push him away, scold him, and if necessary, punch him in the stomach with your knee. Not too hard, but sharply enough to teach him not to do this.

Dear Mr. Riddle:
We have just taken possession of a two year old black Cocker Spaniel. Can you tell me how to ascertain its sex?
Sincerely,
Mrs. _____

The man at the next desk suggested a possible answer, to wit: By silhouette.

Dear Sir:
We have a male dog, and he is always rubbing against people and climbing on their legs. I know what he wants. But where do you take him?
Sincerely,
Mrs. _____

Sir:
Our male dog has never been mated. It would be terrible for him to go through life without, well, you know, at least just once. But how do I go about it, and where?
Sincerely,
Mrs. _____

Alas, there are no dog houses of ill fame, and prostitution is solely a human failing.

Dear Sir:
I would like to find out about getting my female dog spaded. She is a year old. I turn her out for exercise every morning, because I know it is necessary. But I can't watch her and I don't trust her.
I am sick and tired of giving her a douche every time she comes in. And besides, I think she may be getting a fixation on this. How much does spading cost, and will it hurt her?
Anxious Owner
Mrs. _____

Lady, spading is for gardens, and d . . . oh well, see your veterinarian.

Dear Sir:

I have been told that sexual intercourse will make a dog mean. How can this be so? It doesn't do that to people.

Sincerely,

Mrs. _____

But I've heard of crimes of passion.

Dear Mr. Riddle:

My dog is shy. Will mating him give him confidence?

Sincerely,

Mrs._____

No, madam. Only satisfaction.

Dear Sir:

I have been having trouble with the ways and means of my toy fox terror. Many of my friends said toy fox terrors are very easy to understand. But I have found them definentelly the opposite. They are hard to control, sexually, that is.

Would it be possible for you to send me something to explain their ways? Since I have purchased him, I find that they get heated up faster than any other dog I have ever seen.

I would appreciate your effort in sending me some data on this. If you print my letter, please don't use my name.

Sincerely,

Miss _____

Since this is a family type newspaper, I cannot print your letter. As for data, try Dr. Kinsey.

Dear Sir:

I entered my dog in the Novice Class at the dog show, a week from Sunday. Right after I mailed the entry, she got out and got mated to a mongrel.

Does this disqualify her from the Novice Class? Can't I just explain this to the judge?

Sincerely,

Miss _____.

The Novice Class refers only to ring experience.

Sir:

My dog has never been mated. Does this make her ineligible for the American-bred class? And if so, what class should I enter her in? I know they have horse races for maidens.

Yours truly

Miss ⸻

The American-bred class means that the dog was born in the United States of a mating which took place there. At horse races, a maiden is a boy or girl hoss which hasn't won a race.

Dear Sir:

My lovely little female Cocker Spaniel was raped by a big mongrel twice her size, and now she has a litter of pups. The pups are cute, but Taffy has gotten very nervous. I believe the experience of being raped, and then giving birth to mongrels, and caused this.

If I mate her to a friendly Cocker she knows up the street, so that she will have real Cocker pups, will this cure her nervousness? Or do you think this terrible experience will injure her permanently?

Also, if I mate her to this Cocker next time she is heated up, will her pups be Cockers?

Sincerely,

Mrs. ⸻

We have consulted the works of Dr. Sigmund Freud, Havelock Ellis, and Dr. Spock, and we can find no record of sexual traumatic shock in dogs. Cockers mated to Cockers always produce Cockers, regardless of previous matings.

Dear Sir:

I want to have my dog breaded. She is a female fox terror.

After she is breed, what do I do? Will the puppies be borned in 21 days? There is a male fox terror about two miles away from here. But how do I know my dog will like him?

Please answer all these questions because I am an amature.

Yours truly,

Mr. ⸻

Dear Sir:

I noticed in your dog column that you use the word "bitch" to refer to a female dog. This is unfair to female dogs, and I am ashamed of you. Besides, it is an archaic usage. The word, in modern language, is used to refer to an evil and sluttish, or vicious woman, but not to do a dog.

Sincerely,

Mr. _____

Sorry sir! And here I was patting myself on the back for getting the editor to let me use the word to refer to a dog.

Dear Mr. Riddle:

Please tell me where I can send my dog to have him crossed on a female Dachshund. Or if not that, then any female dog. My dog is a two year old Dachshund, with good papers, and he evidentially wants to get mated with something. He follows the children everywhere.

I call up the vet and he said to hit him a couple every time I caught him going through those motions, and he'd learn not to do that. But I can't follow him everywhere all the time.

First he started with my little girl, who is three years old, and now he follows my boy, who is only 2. They'll find out what he's doing any time now. But also, he's getting worse. He'll drag their night clothes off the bed, scratch them into a ball, and then he starts going through that, what you know.

I don't know what you call it, what you do to males like with females. But I guess you know what I mean? Do you? So then you tell me what to do.

Sincerely,

Mrs. _____

You can have your dog castrated. Less drastic measures include dunking in a bucket of ice, whomping the dog as the veterinarian suggested, or waiting for old age to set in.

152

At a dog show near Hollywood, California, some years ago, a sensation was created when two male Cocker Spaniels were found to be locked together in the exercise ring.

The author was judging in a near by ring, and a friend who was nearly in a state of apoplectic excitement, asked that judging cease so that I could witness this startling event. This was done, with suitable exclamations of astonishment.

On the way back to the judging ring, someone (undoubtedly the president of the Florida Chamber of Commerce) was heard to say:

"You see . . . in California even some of the dogs are 'that way' ".

Telephone Call

Caller (a woman):   My dog has mange, and I want you to tell me how to cure it.

Riddle: That would not be ethical. You should take your dog to a veterinarian.

Caller: Well, I'm poor, and I'm on relief, and I haven't got any money to spend. And also, there isn't a vet within two or three miles of me. So you've got to help me.

Riddle: What makes you think your dog has mange?

Caller: I know that's what she has. So you tell me how to cure her. She's broken out, and the places itch.

Riddle: Where is she broken out?

Caller: Well, she's broken out, that's all.

Riddle: But where? On what part of her body?

Caller: Well, she's broken out, I tell you

Riddle: But where? On what part of her body? It depends upon where the breaking out and itching are. It could be mange or eczema. And there are different kinds of mange.

Caller: I tell you she's broken out.

Riddle: But if you don't tell me where, then I can't help you.

Caller: Well, if you must know, it's around her pussy.

153

Telephone Call

Caller (a man): We've got a Dalmatian dog. And as you know They'll eat everything. Now we're in real trouble and we need your help immediately. That dog ate 10 of my wife's birth control pills. Also the cardboard box and the plastic holders for them.

We called one vet and he said the dog could eat 50 of them without harm. But then we called another and he said the dog would die unless we pumped out his stomach immediately.

Now I want to know which one is right and what I should do.

Riddle: I don't know, but I'll find out and call you right back.

Riddle: Is this the Poison Center?

Poison Center: Yes, it is.

Riddle: I'm Maxwell Riddle from the Cleveland Press. A Dalmatian dog has eaten 10 birth control pills. I want to know if these will hurt him.

Poison Center: I'm sorry. We're not allowed to answer questions about dogs.

Riddle: But I've helped you in the past. You should be willing to help me now.

Poison Center: Sorry. We have our orders.

Riddle: Is this the Family Health Center?

F. H. C.: Yes it is.

Riddle: Do you have an expert there on the effects of the so called birth control pills on dogs?

F. H. C.: Well, no we don't. But I think Dr. A. J. Harper is an authority on this. I suggest you call him.

Dr. Harper: That particular brand should have no serious effect on the dog. He might be a little constipated for a few days. And his nipples will swell up. But they'll go down after a few days.

Riddle: But he's a male dog, doctor.

Dr. Harper: I know, but his nipples will still swell up.

The Outcome

The owner of the Dalmatian didn't wait for this information. He had the dog's stomach pumped out. Retrieved were most of the tablets and their containers, a lip stick tube, two rubber bands, and a child's marble. But that wasn't the end . . .

A year later, the telephone rang.

"I'm the man with the Dalmatian. Remember?"

"You mean, the Dalmatian that ate the birth control pills?"

"Yes. Now he doesn't like my wife anymore. He growls at her. Honey, pat the dog."

Apparently he put the receiver down by the dog's muzzle, and I could hear it growling.

"You hear that? What am I going to do with him?"

"Well, where does the dog sleep?"

"Oh, he has a fine bed, with a pillow and everything. And he always sleeps in it."

"Okay. Then tonight when she goes to bed, have your wife put the panties she's been wearing in the dog's bed."

"She doesn't wear panties."

"Well then, have her put any item of clothing which she has worn next to her skin in the dog's bed. That way he will get her intimate body odors. Have her do this for two weeks and then call me back."

Two weeks later, the telephone rings.

"I'm the man with the Dalmatian. Remember?"

"Yes. How did it work?"

"Just great. My wife put her slip and panty hose in the dog's bed every night as you recommended. This was hard on the laundry bill. But it worked. Now the dog loves her dearly and follows her all around the house."

A year later, the telephone rings.

"I'm the man with the Dalmatian. Remember?"

How could I forget?

"Well, the dog doesn't like my wife anymore. He growls at her all the time. Honey, pat the dog."

Growling comes over the telephone.

So now I am really stumped for a solution.

"Mister," I say, "that dog is insane and I can't do anything about it."

"I believe you're right," he says, and hangs up. I never heard from him again.

Dear Sir:

I am beginning to find out that dogs have the queerest sex habits, and my dog must be the queerest of all.

He is a very beautiful Fox Terrier with some Cocker Spaniel and maybe Beagle in him. And he's two years old. What his bad habit is, he actually plays with himself. Like on the children's bed clothes, or sweaters, or any clothing they leave around. Will this hurt him, like with people?

Is there a place where I could take him for sex relief about two times a week? I asked the vet about castorating him, and he said it wouldn't do any good. How come?

> Awaiting your kind help
> Sincerely,
> Mrs. _____.

A clear case of sex on the brain, and it is difficult to remove the brain without hurting the dog.

Dear Mr. Riddle:

I am having troubles with my Beatle hound, and I think you can help me.

He is what you call a monorkit. He has only one testicle. But that is more than he needs. He is a year and a half old. He is always having erections. And he climbs on my little girl's leg and goes through the motions. I don't like to hit him because I know it isn't his fault.

What I want to know shall I have him spaded, or would giving him shots of those female hormones stop those erections. Please tell me what to do. He is a fine dog otherwise.

> Sinceringly
> Mrs. _____

The classic cure is the bucket of ice water. Dunk him bottom end first, of course.

Censorship

A Boxer breeder in the Pittsburgh area spent some time teaching his children the proper nomenclature about dogs. A few days later, his seven year old got up at the Catholic School to talk about her daddy's dogs. She told that they had a three year old bitch which was going to have puppies.

The nun was horrified, and bawled out the child for using such a nasty word. The child duly reported to her father, who explained that only people make the word bad, or out of taste. And that it was always the correct word to use in referring to a female dog.

The child returned to school with this explanation. Later, the father asked his daughter how the matter had come out.

"Fine," said the child, "Sister just said we wouldn't talk about dogs in school any more.

Dear Mr. Riddle:
I have a Great Dane lady and a Dachshund boy. And they are the cutest things together. But now they are in love. Should I let them? And if so, how would they do it? What would the pups look like? And could I sell them, or start a new breed this way? Please answer quickly.

Sincerely,
Mrs. Albert Sanjo

Dear Mrs. Sanjo:
As a boy I had a Great Dane bitch who would run away as soon as she was ready to mate. And she wouldn't come home until she had got mated. I located her once by riding over the area on a horse. Well, she had just backed up on a hillside. But I don't believe that this would work with your dogs. Besides the pups would be something awful with misshapen legs and probably back deformities. You couldn't sell the pups, and in any case, the world is full of unwanted dogs. So the answer is "no," don't try anything.

Sincerely,

Wise Children

Friends of mine were early breeders of Belgian Sheepdogs. They had a daughter who was large for her age. They discussed the matter and decided that it was time to tell the girl some of the facts of life. So they tried to explain to her that very shortly she might begin to menstruate. The girl had some trouble in understanding. Finally, it became clear to her.

"Do you mean that I'll begin to bleed like Suzie (the Belgian bitch) does?"

"Yes," was the reply. "But it will only mean that you are passing from childhood into puberty. You are growing up."

They prided themselves on their success. One Sunday morning they were drowsing in bed when the daughter began to scream. She rushed into the bedroom.

"Mother, Daddy," she yelled in great delight. I'm in heat."

This reminds me of the time I tried to tell my son some of the facts about growing up. I'm afraid I did it not too well. But at the end I did say: "Now, Henry, you play with older boys, and they'll tell you all sorts of things, most of which will be lies. Just come to me, and I'll tell you the truth."

"Yes," he said, "that Peter Ripp has already told me a big lie."

I prepared for the worst.

"What has he been telling you?"

"That big liar said he paid $25 for a second hand bicycle."

I gave up.

Rachel Page Elliott tells this one about her grandchildren. The small boy sat at table, delightedly learning to spit bits of food across the room. He was told to stop but ignored the order. Finally, his older sister shouted at him:

"If you don't stop that Daddy will have you fixed."